MY BOOK OF FIRST FACTS

MY BOOK OF FIRST FACTS

Byeway Books

MY BOOK OF FIRST FACTS

©1985 Posag Establishment 1984

Designed and produced by
Autumn Publishing Ltd
10 Eastgate Square, Chichester, England

This edition published in the USA in 1989 by Byeway Books
Distributed by Supermart Book Distributors, Inc.
A division of BDB Corp.
122 Fifth Avenue, New York, New York 10011

Printed in Belgium

ISBN 0 94659 316 7

Contents

Introduction

Finding Out

The world we live in is a wonderful place. It is beautiful and strange, full of things that we can see every day, such as birds and plants and cars. It is also filled with things that we cannot see, things as surprising as invisible winds that are strong enough to uproot tall trees, and forces such as electricity, which no one sees but which help to make machines work. All of these things affect our lives every day, often in ways that we might not expect. Every young person, and many old ones too, are curious about the world they live in, wanting to know how things work and what they do.

When you see something you haven't noticed before, perhaps an insect on a leaf while you are out taking a country walk, or an unusual kind of stone in the garden, you begin to wonder about it. Sometimes, if you are lucky, you can ask other people for answers right away, but often there is no one near who can tell you the things you want to know. Even if there are grown-ups nearby, they may not be able to answer all your questions, so you have to look for the answers yourself.

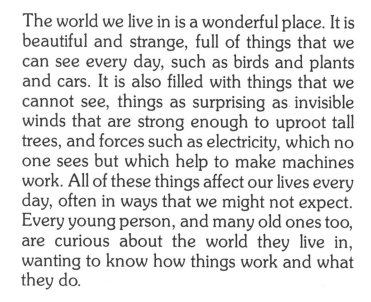

In *My Book Of First Facts* you can find answers of your own to many things that puzzle you. This book will tell you about many of the things you see, and about some of those that you cannot see. It will explain some of the interesting things about countries you have not yet visited, and about times long past when the history of the world was being made by people who were just as curious about their world as you are today.

Long ago, people knew little about the place they lived in. Many of the mysteries that troubled their minds still puzzle us today. We certainly have not found out about everything. But over hundreds of years of learning, people have discovered answers to many of the questions that confused our ancestors. This book explains many of the things that people now understand. Their search for the meaning of things around them has often taken many lifetimes, one generation of people passing on a little knowledge to their children, and those children growing up and searching out more of the truth. We are all part of this great search for understanding the world we live in, and soon you will begin to take your part in this exciting adventure. *My Book Of First Facts* will tell you much that you need to know as you set out on your voyage of discovery of the world's wonders.

At each turn of the page of *My Book Of First Facts* you will find a new story about such things as plants and animals, the way people lived in past times and how they live now. *My Book Of First Facts* explains some of the inventions that help to make our lives easier. Some of these inventions are as old as the wheel and some are as new as space travel.

You can use *My Book Of First Facts* by simply opening it anywhere and starting to read and look at the pictures. If you look at the Contents page at the beginning of the book, you will see a list of the subjects you can expect to find on all the pages; this helps you to choose the things that especially interest you. If you know exactly what you want to find out about, you can turn to the Index at the back of the book. There you will find a list of all the individual pieces of information in the book, with the exact page numbers on which you will find the information.

Opening a new book is an adventure, and *My Book Of First Facts* will lead you to many exciting discoveries.

The Earth's Crust

The Original Cloud — Scientists still do not know precisely how the earth was formed all those millions and millions of years ago. However, by observing what happens among the stars in the universe, some experts believe they can guess that similar events may have taken place when our solar system was formed. These scientists think that there was no sun or plants about five billion years ago. Instead, an immense cloud of gases and cosmic dust whirled around and around. This cloud condensed and formed nuclei. The biggest became the sun. In the beginning, each was white-hot like the sun, some stayed white-hot and became stars then some of them began to cool and became planets.

A Lava Sea — In the beginning, the surface of the earth was an immense sea of molten, steaming lava, into which showers of meteorites and other cosmic matter rained down from space.

The First Crust — It took millions of years for the flaming hot matter on the surface to cool. Where it hardened it formed the earliest rocks. These rocks covered the globe like a crust. It was, however, an unstable crust, continually broken by exploding flames and gases.

The Age Of The Rocks — Our earth was formed from a flaming mass of gas and cosmic dust. It cooled, forming into a solid crusted planet. By studying the oldest rocks with instruments that measure radioactivity, scientists have come to the conclusion that the earth's crust started to form very, very slowly three billion years ago.

A Wrinkled Skin — As it cooled, the earth's size shrank. Like the skin of an old apple, the earth's crust started to wrinkle and buckle. The folds in the surface rock became the first mountains.

The Great Rains — At last the rocks cooled sufficiently so that the water no longer evaporated. The rain began to collect on the ground. It rained continuously for centuries on end, because the atmosphere had to get rid of all the vapor it had accumulated over millions of years. There were terrible floods, and the first seas came into existence. Low ground between the mountains was flooded with rain water, and the rivers wore out their courses along the valley floors, carrying the water downhill to form the oceans.

A Swollen Sky — The white-hot earth hurled dense jets of steam into the air where they formed enormous clouds that completely covered the sky. These clouds turned into rain which fell to earth, where it evaporated quickly in the heat and rose again to the sky. The earth was still far too hot and not a drop of water existed on it.

How Mountains Are Made

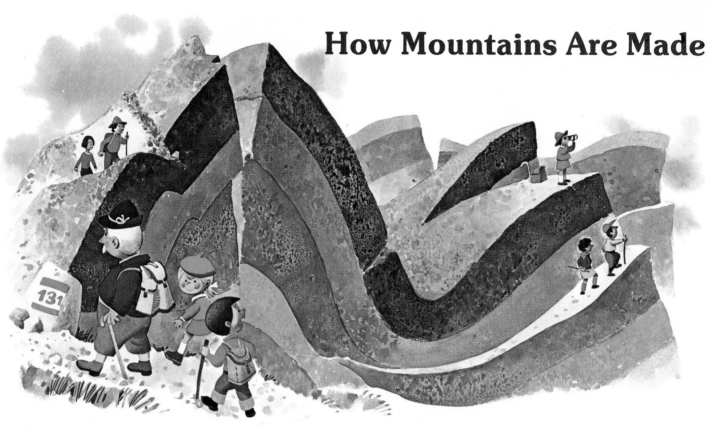

Along Mountain Trails — Let's go for a trip to the mountains. The lovely scenery varies with each bend in the road! But the road comes to an end and you have to follow a path that crosses the fields and goes through the woods, climbing higher and higher as you go. Climbing is hard work but when you've reached the top you can feel pleased with yourself for making the effort. Far below lie wooded slopes and green fields; up here are high, rocky crests. The rock is sometimes formed of uneven strata, or layers. Why is this? To find out, first of all we need to know how rock strata are formed.

How Rock Is Formed — Very often, rock is first formed in the sea. The rivers carry particles of mud to the sea where they drop to the bottom. Shells and remains of tiny marine creatures also settle on the sea bed, and in this way layers are built up. Millions of years later, these particles compress together to become solid rock.

How Rock Bends — Rock is very hard, but under great pressure it will slowly change its shape. When this happens, the layers are thrust upward like layers of cloth being pushed up by your hands.

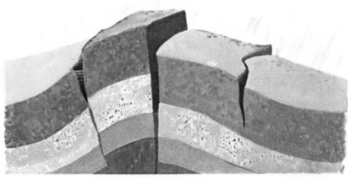

The Bottom Of The Sea — There are mountains at the bottom of the sea. These may be huge mountain ranges that are always hidden in the depths although sometimes a few peaks stick out of the water as islands or reefs.

Valleys And Gorges — Mountains come into existence in other ways too. Rock layers may crack with one section of the rock heaving upward while the other sinks. Later, rain falling on the softer rock wears it away and washes it into the valleys, leaving only the hardest rock still standing.

Mountains of Lava — Volcanoes too can cause mountains to form. Lava may flow from and harden around a huge hole in the ground until it finally turns into a mountain.

Mountains Wear Away — Now you know that mountains are formed by rock layers being thrust upward or breaking, and by lava flowing from volcanoes. It takes millions of years to make a mountain. As time passes, rain and frost eat away at the rock, causing it to split and fall down the mountainside to the valley. This is how stony hillsides, cliffs and valleys are formed.

A Mountain Becomes A Hill — Rain and frost are a mountain's worst enemies. These two elements cause rock to crumble, and the rivers carry the fragments downstream. When this has been going on for millions of years, all that will remain of a great peak are some low hills.

How Fossils Are Made

Rock And Fire — When geologists discover a layer of volcanic rock, they know that great eruptions took place there in the distant past. The area was buried under a sea of boiling lava which hardened into rock.

A Collection — Many children enjoy collecting pieces of rock and minerals. They pick up attractive or strangely shaped pebbles from hillsides or from the bed of a stream. The children clean and polish the pebbles and arrange them in boxes or on special shelves. There are all kinds of rock and many of them are beautifully colored. Rocks are of great interest to geologists, the scientists who study the history of the earth. By carefully examining the rocks, geologists can tell how they were formed, how long ago and why. They can retrace the events that took place on our planet millions of years ago. As far as geologists are concerned, a rock is like an open book. If you learn how to read it, you'll find it contains the whole story of our earth.

This is how the fossil was formed

Rock And Rain — When the rock is composed of grains of different kinds of matter all cemented together, the geologist knows that this area was once under water and that the rain wore away the mountains until sandbanks were formed. This sand also turned into rock.

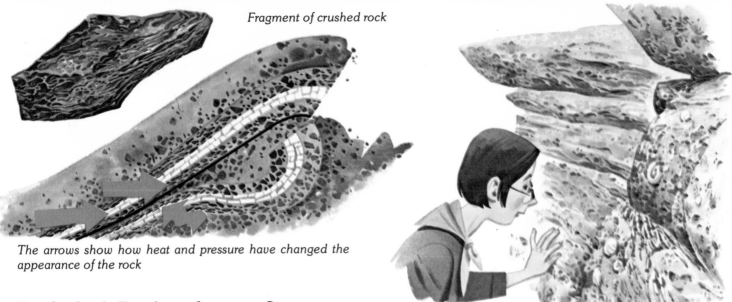

Fragment of crushed rock

The arrows show how heat and pressure have changed the appearance of the rock

Rock And Earthquakes — Sometimes both volcanic rock and sandstone undergo great changes and their grains are flattened into paper-thin sheets. This happened when movement of the earth's crust crushed the rock under a great deal of pressure and subjected it to very, very high temperatures.

Fossils — You can sometimes find the outlines of ancient creatures pressed into the rock. This indicates that when the rock was formed life already existed on earth. The fossils of the plants and animals trapped in the rock as though between the pages of a book, show us what kind of life existed at that time.

The shells embedded in this fossil lay on the sea bed thousands of years ago

Rocks And Animals — Certain kinds of rocks, such as white chalk, are formed from layers of shells belonging to the microscopic creatures that swarmed in the seas when life first began on earth. The geologist knows that when he comes upon chalk rock this was once sea. The mountains were formed at a later stage when the layers of shells which had been hardened into solid rock, were slowly raised and gradually forced upwards.

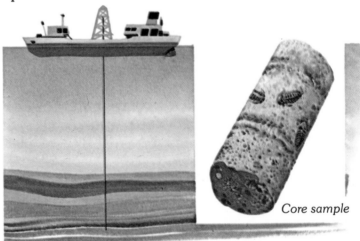

Core sample

Core Samples — Geologists have very advanced methods for learning what deep rock layers are composed of, what they contain and their history. For example, round plugs of rock, known as core samples are drilled out of the sea bed, and from them the composition of underground layers can be studied.

15

What Fossils Show Us

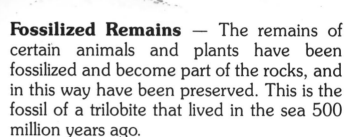

Fossilized Remains — The remains of certain animals and plants have been fossilized and become part of the rocks, and in this way have been preserved. This is the fossil of a trilobite that lived in the sea 500 million years ago.

The Giant — Why is the dog barking and digging in the gravel quarry where the excavators have been moving huge heaps of earth? Today is Sunday, the quarry is deserted and the children have gone with the dog to look around. And what a surprise they get! Scraping away with his front paws, the dog has dug up a bone from the sand. It's very big. In fact, it's a giant bone. It is the shape of a chicken thigh bone — but very much bigger. The animal it belonged to must have been the size of a house! What are the children going to do now? They will dash off and tell the police. Then the experts will arrive and hunt for any other fossil remains of the giant animal hidden in the sand. They will try to rebuild the skeleton and discover what lived in these parts such a long time ago.

Beneath The Sand — Here's the story of the trilobite that we now see as a fossil. When the creature that lived in the sand on the sea bed died, layer upon layer of sand from the surrounding mountains accumulated on top of its body. It became full of mineral salts and turned into stone. Millions of years went by and the layers of sand hardened into rock. Inside lay the fossilized body of the trilobite that had lived so long ago. Gradual movements of the earth's crust pushed these layers above the level of the sea and crumpled them to form a mountain. They split, and part of them sank back into the waves. The trilobite lay very close to the split in the layers of rock. Then the weather-beaten boulder in which it was hidden broke off and crashed down the valley.

A sudden earthquake can uncover a fossil buried thousands of years ago on the ocean bed

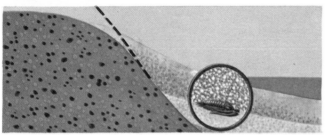

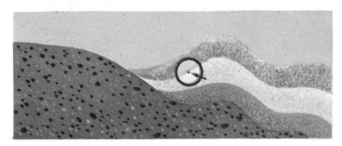

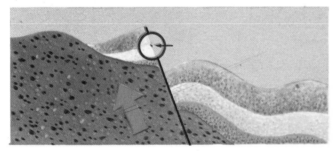

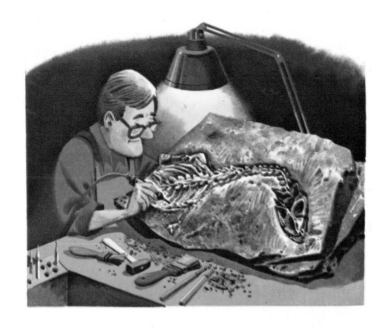

How To Conserve Fossils — Certain fossils are rare and valuable. If you find a fossil, do not try to remove it from the piece of rock in which it is embedded or it will be ruined. If possible, take it to a museum where it can receive expert attention.

In Museums — Thanks to the discovery of fossil remains, experts can reconstruct the animals that once roamed the earth, so we know just what they looked like.

Discovery — One day a climber picked up a piece of rock, saw it had a strange form pressed on it and took it to an expert, who cleaned it and discovered the splendid fossil.

Skeleton of a Triceratops reconstructed for a museum

17

The First Living Things

Shells — You will sometimes find the fossil remains of shells in certain kinds of rock. This shows that the area was once under the sea and that some of the marine animals were buried in the mud on the sea bed, which later turned into hard rock. The sea was the home of the first living things. The rock formed at the bottom of the sea contains fossil remains of ancient creatures and plants which were completely different from those living today. By studying the rock layers containing fossils, scientists have managed to discover what these early forms of life were and something about the way they lived.

Spheres And Ribbons — The primitive inhabitants of the seas at the beginning of time had neither mouth, head or legs. They were just floating blobs of jelly. Then their cells started to unite to form larger and more complex organisms. Millions of years later, sponges appeared and these creatures lived in colonies. Two billion years have gone by, yet many organisms have not changed at all, for instance, sponges. The first octopuses also appeared in these remote times.

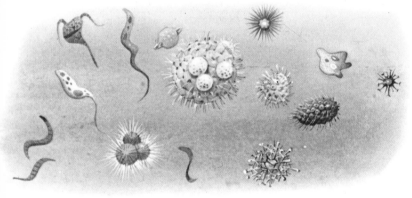

1. *Jellyfish*
2. *Trilobites*
3. *Flat worms*
4. *Onychophora*
5. *Sponges*
6. *Polycheti worms*
7. *Crinoids*
8. *Primitive corals*
9. *Nautiloids*
10. *Sponges*
11. *Starfish and bivalve molluscs*
12. *Scorpion fish*
13. *Horseshoe crab*

The First Monsters
Soft-bodied creatures protected by hard shells began to appear. Some of these had a coneshaped or conical shell. These ranged from small to sizes 12 feet (4 meters) long, and were often brightly colored.

A Curly Shell
As thousands of years passed, the members of the Nautilus family appeared, with their whorled shells. This "house" was easy to carry. Many fossil whorled shells are found in the rocks. Their inhabitants, creatures known as ammonites, were very common.

At The Bottom Of The Sea
The picture above shows what the sea bed looked like about 400 million years ago, after many different species of creatures had evolved. Various kinds of seaweed grew there too. At that time, plants only lived in the sea. Dry land was still completely bare, without even a blade of grass.

The First Fish
The first fish which had backbones made their appearance. They did not resemble present-day fish at all, and most had rigid, ever-open jaws with which they searched for food on the muddy sea bed.

The Plant World

The horsetail

In The Water — Then the plants appeared. First of all, these were tiny floating weeds, which learned to anchor themselves in the mud and later grew roots in order to absorb the mineral salts they needed for food.

Erosion — While the water plants were evolving, dry land was completely devoid of life. Rain wore away the mountains which were not protected by any covering of vegetation.

The Horsetail — These children have found a host of strange plants that look like artificial flowers by the roadside. The teacher explains, "These are plants called horsetails which grow in damp, sandy spots. Nowadays they don't grow very tall. However, many millions of years ago, they grew to a gigantic size and there were entire forests of them." The last descendants of the strange trees that covered the earth millions and millions of years ago are still with us. Even the dinosaurs had not made an appearance then. Plants were totally different from those you see today — their leaves were nothing like leaves are now, nor were their flowers. Trees then resembled giant mosses and ferns. Their common ancestors were the primitive ferns that first evolved in the seas and lakes.

High And Dry — At some point, a number of lakes dried up and the water plants managed to exist without water. Some species settled down very well in their new environment and the land gradually acquired a coat of greenery.

The Flowers — Long after the arrival of the horsetails, some trees began to have flowers and found a new way of reproducing themselves through their ripening fruit and seeds. When that happened, the species similar to those growing today rapidly evolved. This is a cycad, one of the first plants ever to have flowers.

The Forests — With the help of a suitable climate, land plants soon began to evolve and grow to enormous sizes. The first forests, such as this one, began to grow. However, they were nothing like the forests we know today.

Fallen trees form layers; these remains are now our oilfields and coal seams

Hosts Of Fossils — How can we be so sure of all this information about plants of long ago, now that they are all extinct? We can examine their fossil remains in the rocks. When we know the age of the rock, we can calculate the period in which the fossilized plant was alive.

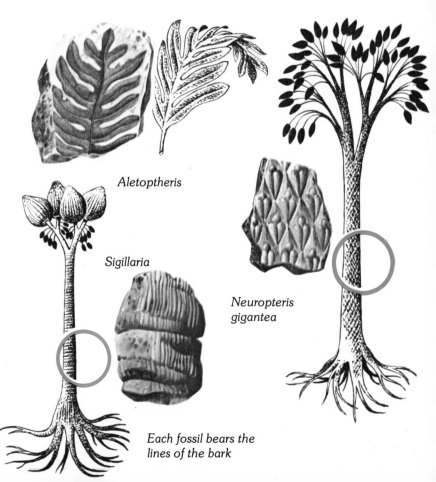

Aletoptheris

Sigillaria

Neuropteris gigantea

Each fossil bears the lines of the bark

Coal And Oil — This was the period, about 300 million years ago, when the huge deposits of coal and oil were formed from the remains of trees and animals buried between the layers of earth or under the sea.

How Plants Feed

Roots — There has been a tremendous storm and the violent wind has uprooted a big tree in the woods. The children are examining the dead giant with its roots torn out of the ground. It has a sturdy trunk and fine spreading branches, but its roots are large and spreading too. What are the roots for? Are they just big underground feet to keep the tree upright?

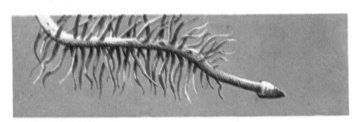

What They Look Like — Roots are different shapes and sizes but they all end in a hard tip which helps to push down through the earth. Each branch of a root is lined with fine threads which absorb the water from the soil. These fine, threadlike roots take up nutritious substances from the earth.

Kinds Of Roots — The most important parts of a root are the little tips that take in food from the soil (and which break when we pull a plant out of the ground). Some roots spread out in a fan, while others push straight down and have few branches. It all depends on the ground they grow in and if they have to push their way around stones.

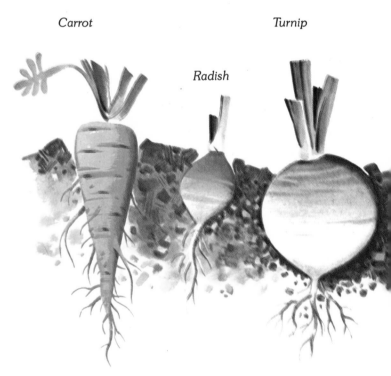

Carrot

Radish

Turnip

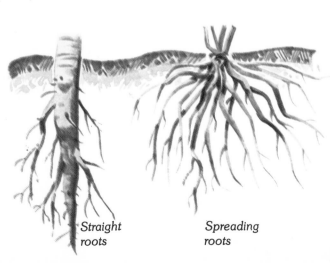

Straight roots

Spreading roots

The Stores — Some roots are very large, even though the plant itself is small. The roots are storing up all the nutrition the plant will need when it awakens in spring, after its winter rest. Carrots, radishes and turnips all have this kind of root.

False Roots — Sometimes under the earth you will find not only roots but thick stems which store food for the plant. These underground stems are called rhizomes. This is an iris rhizome.

Enemies — Many roots, especially the big thick ones full of food, have enemies which gnaw them away. Here are a few pests at work.

Iris rhizome

Daffodil

Onion

Autumn crocus

Bulbs — Certain plants, such as onions, daffodils and crocuses, have enlarged underground leaves. These leaves, full of food for the plant, lie in layers and form bulbs.

Strange Roots — Some roots are not embedded in the ground, like the strawberry runners, the floating roots of water plants, creeping swamp and forest plants.

Strawberry runners

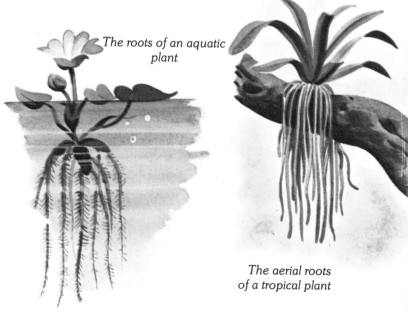

The roots of an aquatic plant

The aerial roots of a tropical plant

Why Trees Have Leaves

The Trees' Covering — In spring, the trees are dressed in green. Their clothes are made of huge numbers of leaves that form a shady, fresh-looking canopy. In summer, the family picnics underneath where it is cool, while the children play in the woods. Here, the children are playing with the leaves and whoever finds the most different shapes and sizes is the winner. It takes a lot of searching, because there are many kinds of trees.

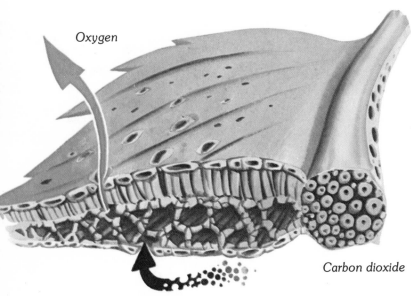

Oxygen

Carbon dioxide

Inside The Leaf — Here is an enlarged section of a leaf. You can see the holes through which the leaf takes in carbon dioxide, and gives off oxygen during the day. This is why where there are plants, the air is fresher as it contains more oxygen. At night the process is reversed, and the leaves absorb oxygen.

Chemical Laboratories — Why do the leaves use the carbon dioxide and produce oxygen? They work just like thousands of tiny chemical laboratories. With the aid of sunlight, they change the water, mineral salts and carbon from the carbon dioxide into new substances which the plant can use as food. When this has been done, the oxygen is discarded and expelled into the air.

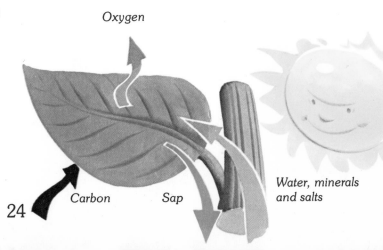

Oxygen

Carbon   *Sap*   *Water, minerals and salts*

Two kinds of palmate leaf

Pinnately compound leaf

Pinnate leaf

Aculeate leaf

Lanceolate leaf

Lobed leaf

Palmately compound leaf

Strange Leaves — Leaves do come in the most peculiar shapes! Some are enormous, like the leaf of the giant water-lily which is the size of a tea tray. Many are very good to eat. Just think of lettuce, cabbage and all the other vegetables we eat.

Why Trees Turn Bright Colors — In autumn, the leaves change color just before they start to fall. The plant or tree has allowed all the refuse that has collected in the trunk during the summer to block the sap vessels, which makes the leaves change color and fall off.

Plants Perspire — As well as the oxygen, the leaves expel tiny drops of water which have been left behind in the process of turning the nutrients into food. In this way, large amounts of moisture return to the air. This is why the climate is not too dry wherever there are lots of trees. The moisture from the leaves rises into the sky to form rain clouds.

Nuts And Berries

Billions Of Seeds — What are these children doing? They are playing with a dandelion clock, but perhaps they don't realize they are helping the plant to spread its seeds and multiply. Each little parachute has a seed attached to it, and the wind will carry it away until it lands on the ground and grows into a new plant. All plants have seeds, some of them inside the fruit, others growing outside in the form of nuts.

Burdock

Chestnut

Acorn

Cherry

Strawberry

Strange Shapes — Seeds come in all shapes, but nature has made each one specially so that it can reproduce the plant far from its parent. Plants always have lots of seeds.

Elm

Poplar

Dandelion

Plane

Lime

Sycamore

Seeds That Explode — Some plants produce their seeds inside oval or round pods, which burst open when the seeds are ripe and scatter the contents far and wide.

Winged Seeds — Some seeds have wings, like those from elm and lime trees, while the dandelion has a parachute head. The seeds of the cotton plant are formed of a feathery material.

Water melon

26

Animal Helpers — Certain seeds, such as those hidden inside fruit, are scattered by squirrels, dormice or birds, which leave them lying on the ground after feeding.

Some spiny seeds spread by sticking to animals' coats

A Sea Voyage — The huge coconut is not afraid of a sea crossing! It falls from the tree when ripe and can float, bobbing up and down in the waves until it reaches a distant sandy beach.

Sowing Time — Since the dawn of history, man has known how to grow or "cultivate" plants by planting their seeds. Here he is, sowing wheat and rice. He also grows vegetables and many other plants.

How Plants Grow

Giants And Dwarfs — Plants such as grass don't ever grow very tall. Trees grow a little taller every year until they reach their full height. Their trunks become huge and we use them as timber. Here some woodcutters are cutting down trees with an electric saw. What a shame! It will take years and years before the young trees grow as high and large as these were.

Climbing Plants — Plants that do not have a woody stem are not sturdy enough to stay erect by themselves and so need support. Look how this beanstalk grows up the cane towards the light. Other weak-stemmed plants climb up walls or around tree trunks. They have many little rootlets with suckers on the ends which hold them in place.

Ivy

Beanstalk

Trunks — Of course, the plants that grow highest and most sturdily are those with woody stems called trunks. See how many different kinds of tree trunks there are in the forests.

28

Refined sap   *Raw sap*

Tubular Stems — If you roll up a sheet of paper, you will see that it is strong enough to support a heavy weight. This is the system the wheat family has adopted — wheat has a thick hollow stem which stands up straight and can take the weight of the ear of wheat.

Invisible Channels — Every stem, weak or sturdy, contains a system of tiny sap vessels, like the veins you see on leaves. These carry the food substances contained in the sap. The raw sap (water and mineral salts) travels up from the roots to the leaves, while the sap already formed makes its way down from the leaves and nourishes the rest of the plant.

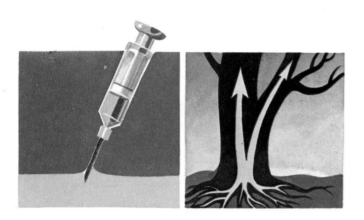

Wood

Paper

Chemical materials

Fabric

How Roots Absorb Moisture — How does the moisture get from the roots to the very top of a tree? By the same principle as liquid sucked into a syringe. It is taken up from below and creates a vacuum in the body of the syringe. In the same way, as the water is absorbed by the roots, a vaccum is created in the little channels throughout the trunk which draws the water upward.

Gifts For Us — Fruit isn't the only gift we get from plants. From tree trunks we obtain timber, paper, material and chemicals for industry. Here you can see a stump. If you count the rings, you will find out how old the tree is, because the trunk grows a full ring each year.

Simple Creatures Of The Sea

In The Water — Let's row over to that half-submerged rock and see what it looks like under the surface of the water. It is crusted with little shells, tube-like shapes and gray marks. Each piece of crusty matter is the home of a tiny creature without a shell that finds the water an ideal environment. Everyone knows there are fish in the sea but not many people realize that the water is swarming with hosts of minute, strangely-shaped living things. They are the direct descendants of the first forms of life that existed on earth.

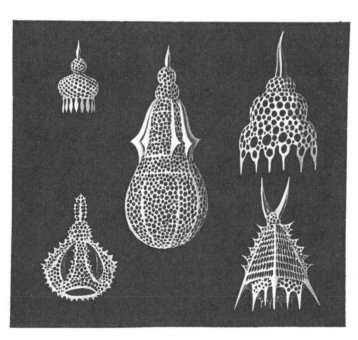

The Radiolarians — Billions of microscopic creatures called radiolarians live in the water. They consist of only one cell and are invisible to the naked eye. Their bodies are covered with a hard lacy armor. This is how they look under the microscope.

False Flowers — There are sea creatures, like the brightly-colored anemones, which look just like flowers on the sea bed. Some worms, such as the peacock worm, have a flowery appearance.

Five Arms — Starfish usually have five arms. They use these to force open shells in order to eat the animals inside. The ancestors of the starfish first appeared on the earth millions of years ago.

Jellyfish — These funny umbrella-like creatures swaying in the water are jellyfish. Some of these species are dangerous because they can give you a nasty sting.

Sponges

The Colonists — Certain primitive sea creatures live in colonies. They link together to form a single body. This body is supported by an external skeleton, which can be either rigid or flexible. Two examples of these linking creatures are the sponges and the beautiful branching arms of coral. Here is a picture of flowering branches of coral: the "flowers" are really tiny creatures leaning out of their holes. The other "tree" has no flowers because the tentacled inhabitants are safe inside.

Corals

Cuttlefish

Sea Shells — Sea shells are very ancient inhabitants of salt waters. There are two basic families: those with curly shells like land snails and those with two valves that open in the middle.

Cuttlefish — Another of the primitive sea dwellers is the cuttlefish, a mollusc with tentacles on its head. Cuttlefish and squid catch fish and other prey with their long clinging arms.

31

Animals That Have Two Lives

Frogs — The children have found a frog on the banks of the pond and they want to see it jump. But the frog is very frightened and crouches down without moving a muscle. It tries to hide in the grass, hoping its green skin will camouflage it from enemy eyes. The other frogs hopped into the pond when they heard the children arrive, and are now in the water. That is what frogs do when they feel they are in danger. They hide at the bottom of the pond, and can stay underwater for a long time without having to come up for air. Like all other amphibians, frogs have two life stages. The first stage is spent constantly in the water. In the second, the frog can live on land as well as in the water.

The Story Of A Tadpole — Frogs start their lives in the water as tadpoles, and for a certain period they breathe through gills, just as fish do. A tadpole would die if taken out of the water. Then its body gradually begins to change: the tadpole grows legs, its tail disappears and lungs begin to develop inside its body. When all this has taken place the adult frog is ready to leave the pond and hop about in the grass looking for insects. Here is a picture of the stages in the life of a frog.

In Ponds And Ditches — Now you know why frogs always live in damp places, never far from water. They need a safe place to hide and, very importantly, in which to lay their eggs as frog spawn is always laid in water.

Toads — This is not a frog but a toad. Toads are also born in the water and start life as tadpoles. Adult toads leave the ponds and ditches and return only when it is time to spawn. Toads are uglier than frogs and have a warty skin. Their faces are flatter and their legs are shorter.

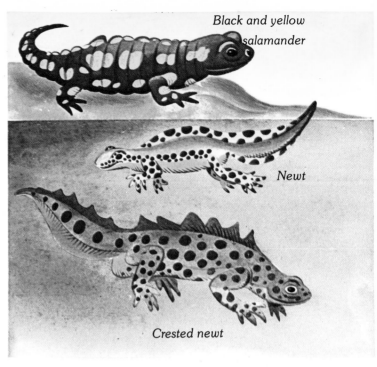

Black and yellow salamander

Newt

Crested newt

A Fine Family — There are many species of frogs in the world. Here are some of the most attractive. As you can see, they are not all green.

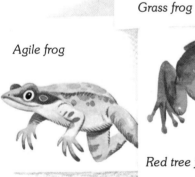

Grass frog

Agile frog

Red tree frog

Newts — These are related to frogs. They look quite different from frogs when adult, but a newt tadpole looks just like any other tadpole.

In Caves — Some amphibians make their homes in dark caves. Below you can see the proteus. It is white because it never comes into contact with sunlight. It is also blind.

Hibernation — Amphibians sleep in the mud during the winter. This is called "hibernation". The cold weather kills all the insects so the frog and its relatives are without food until spring.

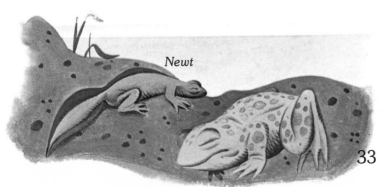

Newt

Proteus

33

Animals That Leave The Water

Frogs — Are frogs land or water dwellers? Well, they're a bit of both. For this reason, we call them "amphibian" which means "with two lives". They spend the early part of their lives in the water, breathing through gills as fish do, then leave the water to pass the rest of their days on land, using their lungs to breathe. The amphibians are the last descendants of some of the first animals to adapt to life out of the water. At the dawn of life on earth, all living things dwelt in the sea as none of them could ever have survived on dry land. They had no lungs to take oxygen from the air and would have suffocated the minute they left the water. However, things began to change and some creatures grew lungs and adapted to breathing in air.

Walking Fish — The population on the dry land began to increase. Certain fish had already adapted to breathing for a short period out of the water, when their ponds dried up and they had to reach other pools in order to survive. Some of them adapted to living on dry land, and these were the first amphibians, creatures with two lives.

The Amphibians — From then on, the amphibians increased in numbers and swarmed over the land. They didn't ever stray too far from water, because they returned to their ancestral haunts to lay their eggs and reproduce.

1. *Eryops*
2. *Dolichosoma*
3. *Icthyostega*
4. *Urocordylus*
5. *Diplocaulus*

Moschops

The First Reptiles — From amphibians, reptiles developed which no longer needed to lay their eggs in water so that their offspring could spend the early days of their lives in the pools. No longer bound to water, the reptiles spread all over the inland regions of the continents.

Fish — In the meantime, fish had been changing. The heavily-armored fish had almost disappeared, and most fish had taken on their present form. Sharks as big as those you find today were already in existence.

Insects — The flutter of wings was now being heard in the primitive forests. The descendants of water scorpions and other species had grown wings and were beginning to take to the air. One of the oldest flying insects is the dragonfly. Some dragonflies had a wing span of as much as 30 inches (half a meter). Birds, however, had not yet evolved.

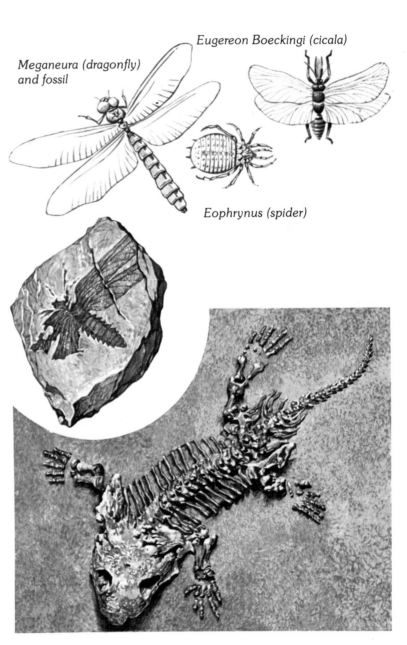

Eugereon Boeckingi (cicala)

Meganeura (dragonfly) and fossil

Eophrynus (spider)

Seymouria Baylorensis

In The Rocks — Fossil remains of all the early creatures that first learned to live on dry land give us information about when and how they appeared.

From the top:
Climatius
Cladoselache
Dipterus
Dinichthys
Cheirolepsis

Prehistoric Animals

The Dinosaurs — Millions of years ago, dinosaurs walked the earth, but very tall tales are often told about them. Though it is true that some dinosaurs were ferocious giants, many others were quite small. Certain species were not much bigger than an ordinary lizard. Even the biggest of them all, those that grew to a length of about 90 feet (30 meters), didn't set any records. Today there are some species of whale which reach a length of 100 feet (33 meters) and no dinosaur ever grew that long.

Museum Specimens — Lots of museums have skeletons and reconstructions of dinosaurs. The remains of these ancient animals are still found from time to time.

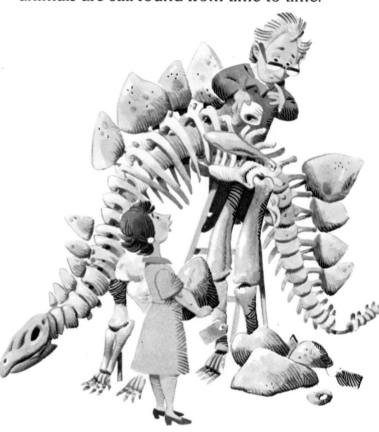

Fossils — How can we be really sure that dinosaurs existed if no one has ever seen one? Our knowledge comes from the fossilized skeletons that lay buried in the ground for millions of years. By patiently putting them together and studying them, scientists have been able to discover what the dinosaurs looked like and the kind of life they led.

The Rocks Talk — By examining the fossils in the rocks, scientists have been able to find out many things. They now know nearly everything about life on the earth before the Age of the Dinosaurs. For example, they are certain that the earliest forms of life appeared in the sea more than a billion years ago.

Brontosaurus

Tyrannosaurus

Diplodocus

Saltoposuchus

Fish And Amphibians — The first living things had no backbone. Fish developed much later and it was a long time before some ancestors of fish began to leave the water and breathe air.

The Reptiles — The first amphibians and early reptiles descended from these ancient fishlike creatures. Then the reptiles spread all over the globe and became the dinosaurs.

Lobefin fish

Seymouria

Moschops

Sky And Sea — Some of these reptiles learned to fly and others went back to the water, where it was much easier to catch fish and molluscs for food.

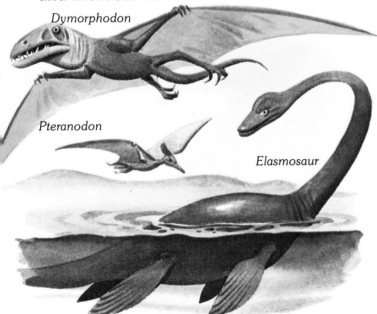

Dymorphodon

Pteranodon

Elasmosaur

Ratlike Creatures — The first mammal forms appeared on the earth much, much later. They were not very large and rather ratlike in appearance. Gradually, other forms evolved to form the different species, right down to the great variety of mammals in existence today.

Ptylodus

Morganucodon

Big Reptiles

Monster — Sailors' legends tell of terrible reptilian monsters as large as whales that rose from the waves. Ships that tried to sail close to them or catch them were smashed and sunk by the furious attacks of these mysterious marine creatures. No one has ever managed to capture one. Some people say that they have seen monsters in certain lakes in Great Britain and Australia. These sound like tall tales, but some scientists think there might be some truth in them after all. These monsters could be the last descendants of the dinosaurs. It is known that giant reptiles walked the earth millions of years ago, but no one knows their true story and the mystery of their disappearance.

Saltoposuchus

Too Heavy — The very large reptiles were the dinosaurs. Some grew so heavy that their legs could no longer take their own weight. They lived near the banks of lakes since movement was easier for them in the water.

Big Reptiles — On Two Legs — The first animals to come out of the water onto the land were amphibians. Later some of these learned to stay out of water all the time and these were transformed into reptiles. Millions of years later some reptiles, small ones like lizards, learned to run fast on their back legs. They used their front legs to catch food and lift it to their mouths; these were dinosaurs.

Plateosaurus

Corythosaurus

Brachiosaurus

Allosaurus

Triceratops

Stegosaurus

The Giants — This is the brontosaurus, one of the biggest dinosaurs that ever existed. It was about 60 feet (20 meters) long and so heavy that the earth trembled when it walked.

Armor-plated — The dinosaurs often engaged in tremendous battles. The meat eating dinosaurs, called carnivores, would attack any kind of prey but often had to fight bitterly to overcome their foe. This was especially true of certain large reptiles with armor-plated bodies. You can see some of these dinosaurs above.

Brontosaurus

Euparkeria

Schleromuchlus Taylori

The Dwarfs — Don't think that all the dinosaurs were giants. Most of them were quite small, the size of lizards or baby crocodiles. In those remote days, 5000 species of reptile inhabited the earth, but only about 100 of these were the giants of our imagination.

The Fishers — Other dinosaurs adapted to life in the water and ate fish.

Tilosaurus

Plesiosaurus

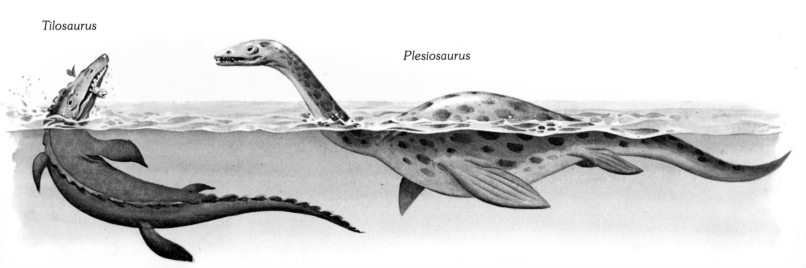

The Insect World

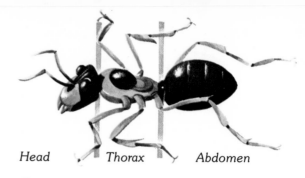

Head   Thorax   Abdomen

Flying Flowers — All children love butterflies and often try to catch them. They don't realize how cruel this is. The minute you touch a butterfly's wings, the beautiful pattern is ruined. The dust on the surface of the wings is easily brushed off and it is this that gives them color. Anyway, what can you do with a butterfly once you've caught it? Either kill it or let it go, when it can hardly fly and is sure to die. It's much better to leave these insects to flutter and dance in the air.

Six Legs — Butterflies are insects as are millions of other tiny living things. All organisms that have six legs are insects, and that is how you can tell this class of creature from others. An insect's body consists of a head, thorax and abdomen. The three pairs of legs are attached to the thorax.

Caterpillar   Chrysalis   Butterfly

Egg

Caterpillars — All insects hatch from tiny eggs and almost all pass through the larval or caterpillar stage before becoming adults. The larva hatches from the egg, grows, turns into a chrysalis and then into the perfectly-formed adult insect.

The Exceptions — Some insects are the exception to the rule. Grasshoppers, for example, look just the same when they hatch, as when they are adults, although they are much smaller. They do shed their skins several times as they grow larger.

Anthill

Wasps' nest

Social Insects — The social insects live in colonies. Each member of the colony has its own job to do, to make the whole community function perfectly. The most wellknown social insects are ants, bees and some wasps.

Beehive

Galls — Many kinds of insect lay their eggs on leaves or under the bark of trees. Some go a bit further. They cause the tree to form blisters or balls, and then they lay their eggs inside these. In this way, the larva is well protected inside the "gall" when it hatches and is also surrounded by its food supply.

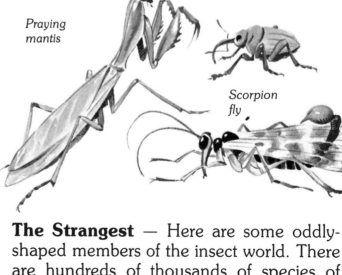

Nut-weevil

Praying mantis

Scorpion fly

The Strangest — Here are some oddly-shaped members of the insect world. There are hundreds of thousands of species of insect on the earth.

How Bees Make Honey

Insect Friends — "Help! I've been stung by a bee!" screams the little boy as he runs away. He doesn't realize that he is unjustly accusing bees of being nasty. Quite often, what we think is a bee trying to sting us. is really a wasp. Unless bees are really frightened, they will not attack people. They are far too busy gathering nectar and pollen from the flowers to take back to the hive. Here is a row of bee hives. They look rather like dolls' houses, but they are real cities, with thousands of inhabitants.

The Honeycomb — This shows the inside of a bee hive. It is full of panels called honeycomb. These panels are cells made of wax. The bees store their honey and pollen in the honeycomb.

The Queen Bee — This queen bee is laying an egg in each of the cells. Every hive has one queen and she may lay as many as 2000 eggs a day. Her attendants are worker bees who feed her with royal jelly. This is produced from the nectar gathered from the flowers and is highly nourishing.

Beeswax — Who makes the six-sided cells that form the honeycomb? This is the job of the workers who produce the wax in their abdomens and then chew it to soften it. While they are doing this, other bees are out collecting the pollen and nectar that will be stored in the cells.

The Sting — Bees do not bite when disturbed or angry, they sting. However, they can sting only once. The sting is on the bee's abdomen. When the bee stings, the little hook on the abdomen is left behind in the victim's skin. By leaving this hook, the bee loses part of his abdomen and dies.

Worker Bees — These worker bees are fanning their wings at great speed to circulate cool air through the honeycombs. Other workers act as sentinels to stop intruders entering the hive. Sentinels are aggressive and are ready to sting anything that comes too close to the hive.

Extinct Birds

Ferocious Birds — When we talk about ferocious creatures, we think of lions, tigers, panthers, jaguars and other carnivorous mammals that attack and devour their prey. No one ever thinks of ferocious birds. Yet some giant birds were far more dangerous than any carnivore that lived on earth millions of years ago. Some species of ferocious birds survived until just a few centuries ago. The first explorers to land on the island of Mauritius, for example, were terrified when they came face to face with the dodo, a fierce bird the size of a bear. The last dodo was killed in 1679. Moa, dangerous, primitive birds taller than an elephant, were found in New Zealand until a few hundred years ago.

Dodo

The Biggest — The biggest of the winged reptiles was the pteranodon. Though its wing span was as much as 21 feet (7 meters) the pteranodon only weighed about 25lbs (12 kilos). It was a strong flier, and could wing for days on end over the sea, diving to catch fish.

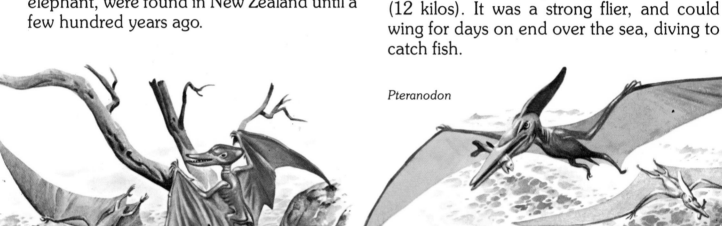
Dsungaripterus

Pteranodon

Winged Dinosaurs — The first flying creatures were not birds at all but small dinosaurs. A thin layer of skin grew from their sides and joined on to their front legs, a bit like a bat's wing. These dinosaurs could glide downward but could not take off from the ground. If they flapped their wings while on the ground, they risked tearing them on stones or bushes. To launch themselves, they had to climb up a tree or on to a rock and then leap into the air.

Feathers — The winged reptiles began to grow feathers, though they still had heads like dinosaurs. These were the true ancestors of the birds that now fly across our skies.

Archaeopteryx

44

A Comparison — Are birds descended from dinosaurs? Have a look at a hen and you'll see for yourself. Just imagine it without feathers and with a slightly longer body. It could quite easily be any one of many dinosaurs that roamed the world millions of years ago.

Ichthyornis

Flightless Birds — The winged reptiles disappeared, giving way to the true birds. The birds began to evolve into a number of species. Some of them grew so big they were too heavy to fly. They adapted well to moving on foot and were able to capture their prey by out-running it. These are the more ferocious and monstrous of these birds, some of them 9–12 feet (3–4 meters) tall, which became extinct not so very long ago.

The Swimmers — Some flightless birds learned to swim and fish. They were very big as well, and are the ancestors of the penguins.

Phororacos

Diatryma

Moa

Cassowary

Emu

Kiwi

The Last Of The Monsters — Strange, flightless birds with primitive features can still be found in certain regions of the world, especially in Oceania. Here are some of the oldest ones.

45

The Bird World

Avocet

Heron

Teal

Grebe

Sky And Water — If we keep quiet and hide, we can watch the birds that live in the marshes. The only way we can study their behavior is to keep out of sight and not move for hours on end. The birds will land only when they are sure there is no danger and they can feed and rest safely. At the slightest sound they will all take flight. Their kingdom is the air and the higher they fly, the safer they feel.

Beaks — Look at the beaks of these birds. The beak is adapted to the kind of food the bird eats. Parrots and crossbills have a sturdy beak for cracking hard nuts. The woodcock has a long bill for prodding the mud. The kingfisher's bill is ideal for fishing and the toucan's for breaking tropical fruit. Short, sharp beaks are perfect for catching insects or pecking corn and tiny insects.

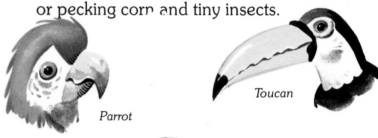

Parrot

Toucan

Woodcock

Crossbill

Kingfisher

Lesser coverts

Secondary and primary coverts

Feathers — How can birds stay up in the air and fly? First, muscular wings. The wings would be useless without down and feathers. It is the wing feathers that spread and enable the bird to remain in the air and to turn and twist in flight.

Colors — Some birds have really beautiful feathers, like the species shown below.

Goldfinch

Blue tit

Golden oriole

Hoopoe

Eagle

Vulture

Falcon

Night Birds — Some birds of prey hunt only at night. They fly quite silently on downy wings. They can see in the dark. They're useful because they kill rats and other pests.

Birds Of Prey — Certain species capture their prey in the air or dive down on it from the sky. Birds of prey have hooked beaks and strong talons. Here are some of them.

Bird Migrations — Each year, some birds set out on long journeys, often from one continent to another. This is to find a warmer climate and more food so that they can nest. Below you can see the formations of some migrating flocks.

Barn owl

Eagle owl

Insect Eaters — All birds are useful, even those that peck the farmer's grain in the fields. Lots of birds are insect eaters. If there were more birds, they would eat all the insects that destroy crops. Then there would be no need to spray insecticides on the crops.

Mallard ducks

Lapwings

The Tiniest Birds — The smallest birds in the world are the hummingbirds. A hummingbird's nest is so tiny it could fit into a spoon. These pretty little birds are found in forests of North and South America.

Wheatear

47

Mammals

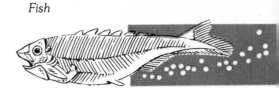

Fish

All From Eggs — Here are some animals that lived on earth before the mammals. All of them laid eggs, either on the ground or in nests. This is the oldest way of reproducing the species, but is not the best.

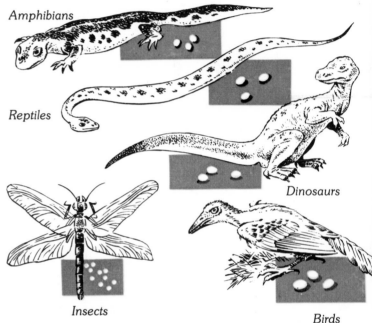

Amphibians

Reptiles

Dinosaurs

Insects

Birds

The Foal — After running happily in the meadow, this foal has gone back to its mother for a drink of milk. The sight of a helpless baby animal with its mother feeding it with her own milk reminds us of our own newborn babies. They both need plenty of care and attention. Indeed, human beings are part of the great family of mammals and need milk when they are first born. Reptiles and the lower animals hatch from eggs and are able to move about and get their own food from the beginning. Although birds hatch from eggs, they need their parents' help at first. However, they are not fed on milk produced by the mother. They all belong to the oldest forms of animal life that appeared when each living creature had to struggle for survival and had no time to tend its young. They laid large numbers of eggs but most of the hatchlings were left to their fate and died almost immediately. Only the strongest survived, ready to face the dangers of life. With the mammals, this was no longer the rule.

Milk Glands — The first animals to give birth to live young appeared toward the end of the Age of the Dinosaurs. The newborn creatures sucked milk, a special liquid produced in milk glands. The first mammals were small and looked like rats. They had two advantages over the huge animals that roamed the earth. They were more intelligent and could move faster.

Morganucodon

Pseudaelurus

Osteoborus

The End Of The Dinosaurs — Shortly after the arrival of the primitive mammals, the dinosaurs vanished from the face of the earth. Some experts think that the early mammals may have contributed to their extinction. The dinosaurs laid their eggs on the ground and left them. Along came the little rodents which ate the eggs before they could hatch.

Small But Fierce — Certain species of very fierce carnivores began to evolve, though they remained small in size.

Ancestors — About 50 million years ago all the ancestors of present day mammals appeared. This was soon after the dinosaurs became extinct. See how the elephant has changed since the days of its ancestors.

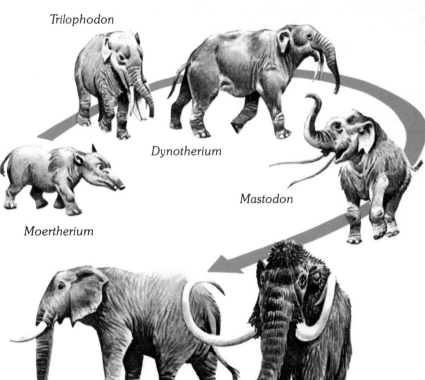

Trilophodon

Dynotherium

Moertherium

Mastodon

The Most Agile — Only the strongest and the most agile animals won the struggle for survival. Certain species have hardly changed at all over the centuries. Others have had to evolve and adapt to their environment. Above are two animals, the Pantolambda and the Barylambda.

Elephant

Mammoth

Early Man

Life — Babies are born every day in the maternity wards of our hospitals. Each newborn baby is placed in a cot and specially trained nurses look after it. When the baby is hungry, the mother gives him or her milk. Several days after the baby is born, mother and baby are ready to go home. This is the way babies today spend their first few days of life, but once it was quite different. Many babies used to die shortly after birth, because they weren't properly looked after. They couldn't be born in hospitals with the aid of nurses and doctors. They lived in unhealthy surroundings and were not well fed.

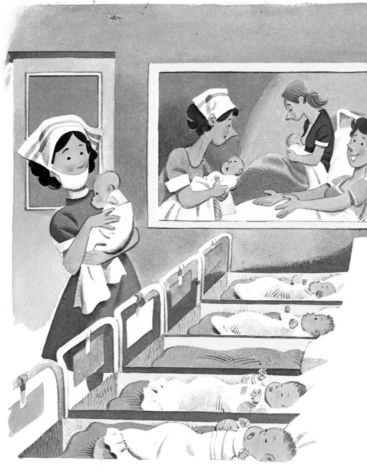

In Caves — At the time of prehistoric man, things were quite different. The mother had to do everything herself. She often had nothing more than a skin in which to wrap her newborn child.

The Midwife — Midwives are highly-trained people who help the mother before, during and after the birth of the child. They work closely with the doctor, although the doctor does not have to be at the birth if everything is going smoothly and there are no complications.

Early Man — Scientists think they know what the first people looked like. Now they are trying to discover how they lived. Fragments of skeletons found in various parts of the world indicate that ape-like people existed two million years ago. The oldest traces of human life come from Africa.

Daily Life — Primitive human beings gathered fruit and berries for food in much the same way as monkeys and apes. Later, they learned to make rough weapons and to trap animals. As the children grew up, they were taken into the forests and taught to hunt.

51

How Clothes Developed

Furs — Man's first clothes were, without doubt, the furry skins taken from the animals he killed. The skins were scraped and cured with salt to make them soft and durable.

Overcoats — This little girl is trying on a new coat in a dress shop. Her old coat is too small for her now, and her mother has taken her to buy another. It is a cold, snowy day, so she must be well covered so as not to catch a cold. "Children that live in hot lands are lucky!" she says to herself. "They don't need overcoats and sometimes wear hardly any clothing at all." But she is lucky, too. She can wear what she wants to keep warm when winter comes. The shops are full of clothes of every kind. Primitive man had never heard of clothes, and keeping warm was a serious problem.

Needle And Thread — Single skins from small animals would not cover a person's body adequately. The villagers learned how to sew the skins together using bone needles and plant fibers or animal tendons for thread.

Climate — What was the climate like on earth when the first people appeared? It was not the same all over the globe. Some regions were very hot. Others were very cold and the inhabitants had to protect themselves against the bad weather. Early man had to use his wits to find something that would keep him warm.

Wool — Some time later, someone began to braid together tufts of wool torn from sheep and goats. This was the beginning of spinning. However, this sort of thread was still only used for sewing, or to make ropes.

Spindle

Bobbin

Weaving — By this time, the tribespeople already knew how to weave. They used canes or reeds and wove them into baskets and mats. The first fabrics were probably created when someone tried to weave woollen threads together. This was a vital discovery, for it meant that furs were no longer the only material for making clothes.

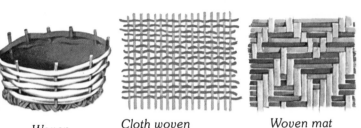

Woven canes

Cloth woven the same way as cane

Woven mat

This is how plant fibers were treated

Beaten out   Dried

The plants were left to soften in water

Combed . . .

to obtain clean fibers

Plant Fiber — Our early ancestors also learned how to obtain fibers from plants. Certain plants, such as flax, hemp, and cotton, provided fibers that were soft and strong. These fibers were ideal for spinning.

The Loom — The art of fabric weaving spread rapidly. Soon all the villagers were doing it. A primitive loom was invented to keep the threads tight, making the weaving easier and quicker.

Mortar for pounding colored earth

Squeezing the juice of wild berries

Dyeing — No longer content with warm fabrics to protect him from the weather, man now wanted clothes to look attractive, too. He learned to color them with juices from plants and other natural dyes. This is how the first colored fabrics were made.

Leather — Skins were never abandoned. They were now used as a source of leather. Their principal uses were for making sandals and different utensils for use in the home and at work.

The Wonder Of Heat

Fire — It was a great day when early man learned how to control fire. The leaping flames gave more heat than the sun's rays. For a long time families huddled round the fire and warmed themselves by the flames on cold, wintry days. However, as time passed, they realized that fire had other uses as well.

Cooking — The first wonderful thing they learned to do with fire was to cook their food. Meat, vegetables and cereals kept longer, tasted better and were easier to digest after they had been cooked.

Pottery — By "firing" the clay pots and vases in a huge fire, pottery was more durable. This invention meant that there were now many kinds of pots for use in the hut and at work.

Metals — When certain kinds of rock were put into a very hot fire, the metals contained in them could be extracted. These metals could then be shaped while they were still hot.

The arrows indicate the flow of hot air

Heating — It was a great achievement to succeed in making heat circulate inside houses so that every room was warm and comfortable in winter.

Heat from the burning wood rises and flows under the floor. Roman houses were heated in this way

Metallurgy — Nowadays, vast metalworks do nothing else but treat and transform metals using powerful heat.

This works makes use of natural heat to produce energy

The very high temperatures in this blast furnace forges this steel bar

Volcanoes — Even the heat that comes from the depths of the earth is being used to produce energy. Water is transformed into steam which is then used to power the large machines which produce electric currents.

Early Fruits And Vegetables — Heating greenhouses means that fruit and vegetables can be produced at any time of the year and not just in summer.

Ice — Man has mastered heat so thoroughly that he can extract it from substances by cooling them. By taking away the heat from the water inside a refrigerator, he obtains ice.

Internal heating in a greenhouse

These plants bear fruit because the heat inside the greenhouse is kept constant

The Invention Of The Wheel

Sledges — Every time a hunter killed a big animal, he had to get it back to the village. Since the carcass was far too heavy to carry, he invented a rough kind of sledge by chopping down a thick, leafy branch. He hoisted the dead animal on to the foliage. Then he grasped the thick end of the branch and dragged his prey back to the huts.

On A Hillside — These woodcutters have felled some trees, lopped off the branches, sawn up the trunks. Now they are rolling the timber down the hillside to the valley. This saves much hard work. Even early man knew that it's easier to move a heavy object by rolling it rather than pulling it.

The need to find a solution to practical problems has always driven man to new inventions, such as the wheel which was probably first thought of when man watched tree trunks roll downhill.

Rollers — It is quite likely that, while rolling tree trunks down hillsides, early man thought of using wooden rollers to help move boulders and other very heavy objects. Plenty of willing hands were still needed to pull the load and shift the rollers to the front so that it was kept moving. These rough rollers were the forerunners of the wheel, one of the most important of all early discoveries. It revolutionized a whole way of life.

The Mystery Of The Axle — One day, nobody knows when or how, it was discovered that it was not necessary to shift the rollers under the load. The load could rest on fixed supports linked to an axle and a pair of circular blocks of wood which went round at the sides of the load. The first wheel had been invented.

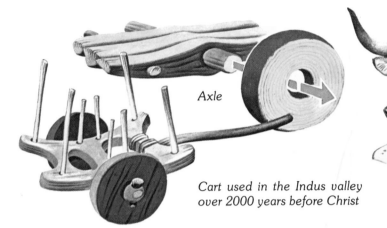

Axle

Cart used in the Indus valley over 2000 years before Christ

Carts — A long time was to pass before proper wheels were built. Once this was done, carts soon followed. This saved a great deal of hard work when heavy loads had to be transported.

Draught Animals — By the time carts were first being constructed, man had been raising livestock for a long time. It was natural that he should use his oxen or donkeys to drag this new wheeled vehicle.

The Spokes — The first wheels were made of solid wood. When man decided he wanted lighter vehicles that would travel more quickly he tried to reduce the weight of the wheels by cutting holes in them. In time, he learned to make spoked wheels, which were much better and lighter.

The Roads — Before the coming of wheeled vehicles, roads had never been needed, but carts could not travel over rough ground or through the forests. Forest tracks had been quite adequate to travel on before. Now, however, some kind of wide, beaten surface had to be made for the carts.

All Kinds Of Work — Wheels turned out to be useful for many purposes. A huge wheel armed with pails placed in the river enabled man to draw water and pour it into fields to irrigate the crops. The potter's wheel, water mills and many other kinds of primitive machines were invented after the discovery of the wheel.

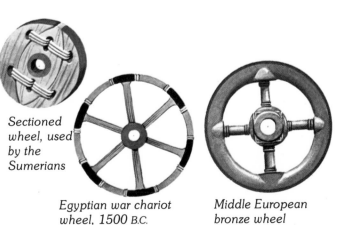

Sectioned wheel, used by the Sumerians

Egyptian war chariot wheel, 1500 B.C.

Middle European bronze wheel

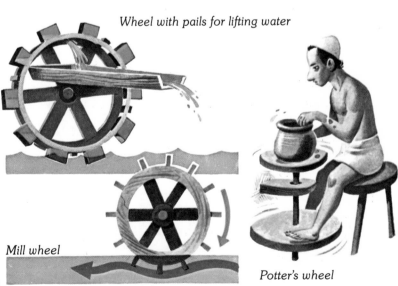

Wheel with pails for lifting water

Mill wheel

Potter's wheel

57

Metal

In The Village — This is probably what a primitive village looked like in the days when men first began to understand how to smelt metals. Metals are not often found in a pure state, but are usually mixed with earth and rock, called ore. For this reason, thousands of years went by before men discovered metals and learned how to extract them from their ores. Some villages, like this one, had inhabitants who were clever at extracting pure metals from ores. They did not keep all the metal but used it to barter for food, skins and other objects.

Copper — As he made up his fire one day, a villager found lumps of reddish-yellow metal, not unlike gold. These were lumps of copper. Copper ore had been left near the fire and become hot. The metal inside had melted and flowed out onto the ground. Once the fire went out, the metal cooled and hardened again.

Gold — Of all the well-known metals, gold is the only one found in a pure state in nature. It may well have been the first metal known to man. Gold is a very soft metal. All man had to do was hammer it in order to shape ornaments and jewelry from it.

Copper ore

Weapon Heads — Copper ore is always a blue or green color. Once man realized this, he found it easy to find the ore and heat it to obtain copper. However, molds had not yet been thought of and man had to beat the metal with a stone to get the shape he wanted. In this way, he made sharp heads to lash to his spears, arrows, hooks and other weapons and tools.

Spear head

Harpoon

Ax

Hook

58

Bronze

Bronze — It was easy to work copper, because it was a soft metal. Then one day it was discovered that when copper ore was melted with another kind of rock (which contained tin) a much harder metal was obtained. Ancient man had discovered how to make bronze. With this mixture of two metals, his weapons and tools were much more efficient.

The three sections of an ax mold   *The molten bronze is poured into the mold*   *The ax is then hammered*

The First Mold — One day, as he was melting copper ore, a man noticed that when the molten metal ran into a hollow in the ground, it hardened there in the same shape as the hollow.

The Clay Mold — If the copper ran into a hollow in the shape of an ax head, a copper ax head would result without having to beat the metal. The man took a block of soft clay, pressed his stone ax head into it and left the impressed clay where the flow of copper would run into it. After the copper had hardened, the man broke off the clay mold and found the first molded ax head in his grasp.

In this picture you can see an early bronze ax; tools and weapons made of this alloy were much tougher.

Iron — Many centuries passed before men discovered iron. A very high temperature was needed to melt the metal from the iron ore. In fact the ore had to be reheated a number of times to extract the metals.

These tools from different European countries show the progress made in smelting and shaping metals. The rough primitive axes gave way to tools forged with amazing skill, considering the scarce means available to early metalworkers.

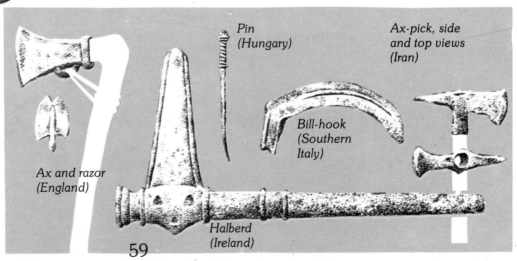

Ax and razor (England)

Halberd (Ireland)

Pin (Hungary)

Bill-hook (Southern Italy)

Ax-pick, side and top views (Iran)

The Pharaoh Cheops

King And Priest — Cheops lived nearly 5000 years ago. He was one of the most powerful rulers of ancient Egypt. These rulers were known as Pharaohs. While people in other parts of the world were living in caves or miserable huts, Cheops owned a splendid palace. He had an army of slaves and thousands of servants at his command. His subjects looked on him as the son of the god Amon-Ra and were ready to obey his orders and those of his ministers without question. The Pharaoh was rarely seen in public for he left the palace only for the most important religious ceremonies. When he passed, he was escorted by a procession of high officials and priests. The people bowed to the ground in adoration.

The Great Pyramid — Cheops ordered the greatest pyramid in Egypt to be built for him. This immense monument was his tomb. His embalmed body was to be laid there.

The Slaves — Thousands and thousands of slaves labored to build the pyramid, carrying the blocks of stone from the quarries and building them up until the construction rose into the air.

Mummies — The ancient Egyptians believed that after death the soul went to live in another world. The body of an important person was embalmed, turning it into a mummy, and buried inside a large tomb. Precious objects and food were left with it for the journey to the next world.

In Battle — Cheops extended his kingdom beyond the reaches of the Nile river. When the nomads of the desert beyond the Red Sea rebelled, he sent an army to punish them mercilessly.

The Queen — The Pharaoh's wife was very powerful too. She had many handmaidens who made her splendid clothing, perfumes and beauty creams. Privileged women like the Pharaoh's wife used a lot of make-up, especially on their eyes.

Cleanliness — The Egyptian men and women paid great attention to bodily cleanliness. They took a bath nearly every day and massaged creams and delicate perfumes onto their bodies.

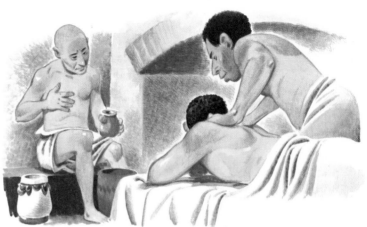

Medicine — Many skilled doctors and their pupils thronged the court of Cheops. Some of them were capable of carrying out difficult operations even though their instruments were still rather primitive.

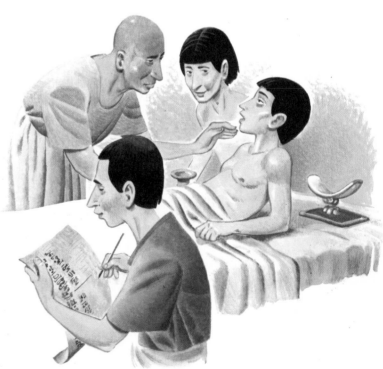

Writing — Hieroglyphics was the name of the writing system. It was devised before Cheops. Instead of printing letters the hieroglyphics consisted of tiny pictures. These were arranged in vertical columns.

Julius Caesar

The Victorious General — The greatest of all the Roman generals was Gaius Julius Caesar. He was brought up in a noble Roman family. Being young, ambitious and blessed with a keen intelligence, he chose a military and political career. He knew he would have an excellent future ahead of him. He fought for many years against the barbarians, extending the frontiers of the Roman Empire as far as Germany and England, and pushing into Africa and Asia. He used 100 armies in the campaigns. He was also a great writer. His most famous work was about his battles in Gaul. But he also had many enemies among his fellow countrymen. They were jealous of his success. He also had to fight against them in a long civil war. Finally he triumphed over everyone and became the sole ruler of Rome. He governed wisely and promised the people several reforms, but many still hated him.

Ambition — Caesar was accused of having too much ambition. Yet in spite of his errors, he was highly sensitive to the needs of the Rome he loved and, whenever he could, passed reforms improving the life of the Romans.

In Gaul — Caesar's qualities as a great general showed to the full when he led the Romans to conquer Gaul (present-day France) and the lands inhabited by the Germanic tribes.

In Britain — After Caesar conquered the Gauls, Helvetians and Bretons, he crossed the sea to Britain. Roman rule was then spread to the part of Britain that is now England.

Vercingetorix — Caesar had to hurry back to Gaul because a rebellion had broken out. The rebellion was led by a courageous man called Vercingetorix. The Gauls were beseiged in the city of Alesia. They put up a brave resistance but were eventually forced to surrender. Caesar took Vercingetorix prisoner and brought him to Rome.

Cleopatra — During the civil war, Caesar went to Egypt and there met the queen, Cleopatra. He married her and brought her to Rome. After his death, Cleopatra went back to her own kingdom.

The Conspiracy — Caesar had been warned many times to be careful. Someone wanted him dead. But he paid little attention. One day a group of conspirators surrounded him and stabbed him to death.

Against Rome — The Senate in Rome feared that Caesar was becoming too powerful. It ordered him to return to the city without his army. But Caesar arrived in Rome with his own men. The Senate surrendered to him and Caesar became the sole ruler of all Roman territories.

Attila The Hun

Attila was leader of the Huns, a nomadic people

King Of The Huns — The ancient Romans called all those people who lived beyond the borders of their Empire barbarians because they thought them rough and uncivilized. But powerful civilizations flourished outside the Roman Empire, even though their customs were different from those of Rome. Most of these people were nomads or wanderers. Because they were always moving, they had no need for cities with buildings and palaces. They were intelligent and brave, skilled horsemen and wonderful archers. One of the most powerful of all the barbarian tribes was the Huns. When Attila became their king, they were already masters of vast territories, including the Roman Empire in the east. Attila was thirsty for more, and he decided to conquer the west and take Rome. By this time, the barbarians felt that they were stronger than the powerful Roman armies.

Honoria — Honoria provided an excellent excuse to march against Rome. She was the sister of the Roman Emperor, who had imprisoned her in a tower. Honoria sent a message to Attila. She would become his wife if he would set her free.

Negotiations — Attila considered himself as good as married to Honoria. He ordered the Emperor, Valentinian III, to set the princess free and give her half the Empire as a dowry. If this was not done, Attila would declare war.

The First Invasion — Because the Emperor sent no reply, Attila and his men invaded Roman territory. They conquered Gaul and destroyed many of the towns. Attila was defeated at the terrible battle of the Catalunic Fields.

The Huns were always on the move and so never constructed cities with palaces and monuments

Cities Ablaze — Attila retreated to Germany. The next year he swept back into Italy to take his revenge. He burned and razed to the ground every town in his path. Even ancient Aquileia was destroyed by the Huns.

Pope Leo — It seemed that nothing would stop the advancing Huns. Yet Pope Leo I faced Attila unarmed and persuaded him to go back to Germany.

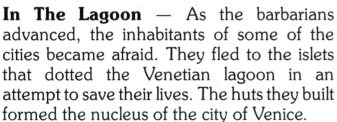

In The Lagoon — As the barbarians advanced, the inhabitants of some of the cities became afraid. They fled to the islets that dotted the Venetian lagoon in an attempt to save their lives. The huts they built formed the nucleus of the city of Venice.

The End — Nobody knows why Attila agreed to retreat. Perhaps his men were tired. Attila himself died only a few months later. He was 58 years old.

Richard The Lionheart

The Crusades — The Moslems were followers of the prophet Mohammed. They had conquered the places where Jesus Christ had lived. These were sites that Christians held sacred. Christian pilgrims to Jerusalem were often ill-treated and robbed by the Moslems. The Pope asked the Christian kings of Europe to fight the Moslems in the Holy Land and free Jerusalem and the Sepulchre of Jesus. Many did as the Pope had asked. These expeditions were called the Crusades. They set out under the Cross of Christ. Jerusalem was won and lost, not once but several times. This was mainly because the Christians never had a leader who was capable of commanding all the armies. Another reason was because many nobles ventured to the Holy Land in search of riches rather than as an act of faith. A number of kings took part in the Crusades, which lasted for 200 years. One of these kings was Richard I of England, known as "the Lionheart" for his courage.

The Journey — As soon as he became king, Richard sold all his possessions and emptied the coffers of the realm to finance an expedition to the Holy Land. He took a large army with him when he set sail.

The Storm — Richard's journey to the Holy Land lasted for more than a year. The ships were blown off their course to the island of Cyprus. Cyprus was then a part of the empire of Constantinople. Richard conquered the island and went on his way.

Taken Prisoner — When he reached Austria, he was recognized by an enemy prince and thrown into prison. Two years later he was set free after paying a ransom of a hundred thousand gold sovereigns.

A Shower Of Stones — When he arrived in the Holy Land, Richard helped the other crusaders to capture Acre. They built large war machines that rained stones on the city. Victory was theirs.

Home Again — Richard returned secretly to England. There he made himself known to his loyal followers and overthrew his brother, John. But John was not the only person who stole power from Richard. Philip Augustus, King of France, had always plotted against him. While Richard was away, Philip Augustus had seized some of Richard's lands in Normandy. Richard landed in France and fought Philip Augustus for a long time. One day, during a seige, he was hit by an arrow and died.

Saladin — The fame of Richard's courage spread to the enemy camp. Saladin, the supreme leader of the Moslems, had a great respect for him. He even sent food and medicine when he learned that Richard was ill.

A Secret Return — Richard did not succeed in retaking Jerusalem. He was warned that his brother was plotting to become king of England. So Richard left secretly for home, dressed as a pilgrim.

Genghis Khan

An Orphan — Temugin's father was a tribal chief who was poisoned by his enemies when Temugin was only 13 years old. Temugin found it difficult to inherit the chiefdom at that age. However, he was strong and courageous and soon was recognized by his own and other tribes to be a great leader.

Without A Palace — Genghis Khan was one of the most powerful rulers that ever lived, yet he didn't even have a permanent home. The leader of a nomadic people called the Mongols, he spent his life on horseback and slept in a tent. The Mongols grazed their flocks and raided where they could, each tribe fighting against the next. Genghis Khan united the tribes and led them to conquer almost all the lands they knew about. As a young man, Genghis was called Temugin and the story is that, while the Mongol chiefs were gathered in a wood to acclaim him as their ruler, they talked of what he should be called. Suddenly a lark began to sing "Gen-ghis, gen-ghis" as it winged into the sky. "Do you hear that?" asked a high priest. "This is the wish of the gods." And so they called him Genghis, the all powerful. In the Mongol language, Genghis Khan means "the most powerful of leaders". And that he certainly was.

A Prisoner — Genghis Khan led the Mongols in their many battles which they always won. One day he was wounded, though not seriously. The enemy warrior who had inflicted the blow had been captured, and was led before him. Instead of killing the man, as everyone expected, Genghis Khan appointed him captain in his army as a reward for the courage he had shown.

The Great Wall — Genghis Khan decided to invade China. With an army of 200,000 men, he advanced over the Great Wall, destroying towns and cities until he reached the capital.

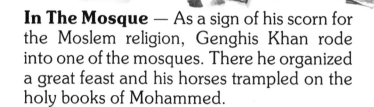

In The Mosque — As a sign of his scorn for the Moslem religion, Genghis Khan rode into one of the mosques. There he organized a great feast and his horses trampled on the holy books of Mohammed.

Peking In Flames — Peking withstood the siege for a long time, but was forced to yield. The inhabitants fled, the Imperial palace burned for a month and the whole capital lay in ruins.

In Russia — Some of his generals thrust forward into Europe and conquered parts of Russia. Genghis ordered them to return home, for he had too much territory over which to rule already, and also had to cope with rebels in the east.

The Fall — Back in his native steppes, the Khan tried to unite his empire even more closely. But one day he fell from his horse and was injured. He did not recover from his injuries and died without anyone to succeed him.

Against The Arabs — With China under his rule, Genghis turned to the conquest of the Moslem empire, which at that time was immensely powerful. His hordes killed fifteen million people before they could conquer all the Arab cities.

69

The Discovery Of America

Christopher Columbus

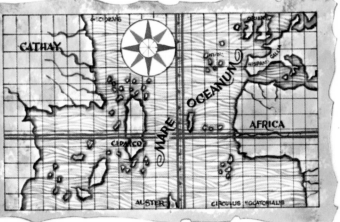

The Shortest Route — When people realized the world was round, certain scholars were sure that the unknown part of the earth was covered by oceans. They thought that if a ship were to sail westward, it would reach the Indies on the other side. This would turn out to be the shortest route to the rich lands from which ships returned laden with spices, precious stones, silks and other fine articles. A navigator called Christopher Columbus decided to attempt this voyage. With aid from Queen Isabella of Spain, he sailed away with three ships. However, he did not know that he would find his route blocked by an enormous continent, which we now call America. When Columbus landed there, he was convinced he had set foot on the Indies. A little later, another explorer called Amerigo Vespucci proved that the newly-discovered lands were in fact a new continent. He described them so clearly that people in Europe began to call them "Amerigo's lands", and from this came the name "America".

Caravels — Columbus set off across the great mysterious ocean in his three small caravels. Three months later, he landed in what is now Central America, but he was sure he was in Asia.

The Indians — As a result of Columbus's mistake, the native populations of America are still called Indians, for Columbus was sure that they were the natives of India.

Cortés — After Columbus many other explorers crossed the ocean to conquer American soil in the name of the kings of Spain. With 500 men Hernando Cortés invaded the Aztec kingdom, in present day Mexico and destroyed its splendid cities, carrying off the vast quantities of gold belonging to their inhabitants.

Balboa — The first explorer to land on the coast of the Pacific Ocean, near Panama, was Vasco de Balboa. Of the 190 men he started with, 133 were killed by natives or died of tropical fever while crossing the vast forest.

Cabral — Pedro Cabral, who was in the service of the King of Portugal, discovered Brazil after a long voyage with 13 ships. This is why Portuguese is still the language of Brazil.

Strange Creatures — The explorers came across many strange creatures they had never seen before during their adventurous travels, such as parrots and the tapir.

New Plants — They also brought new foods to Europe; vegetables such as the potato, tomato and maize were introduced as well as exotic fruits.

Pizarro — In 1533 Francisco Pizarro conquered the mighty Inca empire of South America, in the name of Spain. The Spanish Conquest was one of dreadful massacre and plunder.

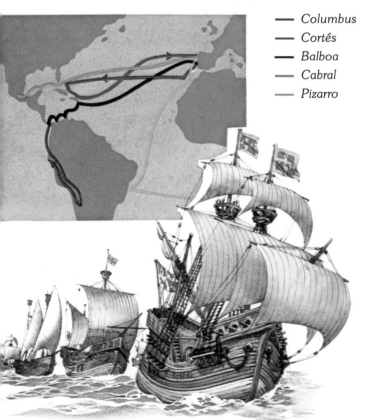

— Columbus
— Cortés
— Balboa
— Cabral
— Pizarro

71

Catherine The Great

The Russian Empire — Of German origin, Catherine married a prince of the royal family of Russia and became Empress by deposing her husband, Peter III. She was very ambitious and cultured and wanted to make the Russian Empire the most important in Europe. Barely 100 years before, Russia had been a land of warriors, nomads, peasants and quarrelsome nobles. Then a great prince, Mikhail Romanov, seized power. His successors set about imitating the methods of government of other European rulers and entered into alliance with them. French was the fashionable language at the Russian court and works of art, good books and fine music were all enjoyed. The Czar (Emperor) brought architects from the capitals of Europe to build magnificent palaces for him. Philosophers and men of culture lived at the Court with every honor heaped upon them. But though the splendor and riches of the Court increased under Catherine, she had to face the discontentment of the population, especially of the peasants who lived in poverty. Catherine wanted to expand her already vast territories. She agreed to share Poland with Frederick the Great.

Peter III — Grand Duke Peter was neither handsome nor intelligent. Instead of learning how to rule, he amused himself by playing with his puppets or inventing war games with his servants. But the young German girl could not refuse to marry him. Apart from that, she also dreamed of becoming Empress and ruling over all Russia.

A Messenger — As a girl, Catherine was called Sophia Augusta Frederica and her home was in Germany. She was related to the Russian royal family and was chosen to be wife of Grand Duke Peter, the heir to the throne. One day, a messenger arrived from Imperial Russia, telling her to leave immediately because the prince was waiting to marry her. Though taken by surprise, Sophia faced the long journey bravely.

At Court — Sophia patiently tolerated her husband's faults and learned to speak Russian fluently. She became a convert to the Russian Orthodox Church and was rechristened Catherine. She learned how to behave at Court, to deal with ministers and ambassadors and became a friend of many important men, including the army generals.

The Nobles — In order to win the friendship and support of the nobles, Catherine granted them many privileges. The peasants and poor people, however, who had to do all the hard work and bear the burden of taxation and misery, were given nothing in return.

The Plot — When her husband became Emperor after the death of his mother, Catherine knew exactly what to do. She waited until the Czar was absent from the capital then, with the aid of a number of generals who were loyal to her, she proclaimed herself Empress. Dressed in the uniform of an officer, she mounted her horse and led her men against the Imperial Guard. There was no need to fight, for the Emperor signed his abdication and mysteriously died shortly afterward.

The Revolts — The people were thoroughly discontented and many revolts broke out, all suppressed with bloodshed. The most famous was the peasant's revolt, led by a man called Pugacev, which lasted for 18 months.

Reforms — Catherine passed many reforms, however, expanding trade and founding new cities. She also enabled women (though only those of noble birth) to go to school, and encouraged education. During her reign, Russia became a powerful country.

73

George Washington

The United States — The capital of the United States bears the name of Washington, after a great general who led the struggle against the British and achieved independence for the American settlers. He was the first president of the new nation. In 1775 the North American territories were considered colonies of Spain, France or Britain. The British had thirteen colonies, but the white settlers had fewer and fewer ties with Britain, and representatives of the Government made an appearance only to collect the taxes. Indeed, it was extreme discontent over taxation that led the settlers to assemble and protest, and finally it was agreed that the time had come to break free of British "protection" and declare the revolution. George Washington was appointed leader of the settlers. One year later, representatives of the thirteen colonies proclaimed the United States of America independent from Great Britain. This took place on July 4, 1776. For another five years Washington and his army fought against the British troops who had been dispatched to suppress the rebels. However, the new American army of the United States, helped by the French who had territories in neighboring Canada, won the struggle.

In The Forests — Washington was born into a rich, Virginian landowning family. He had an adventurous youth, living for years in the forests and mapping unexplored regions.

His First Enterprise — Washington became an officer in the British colonial army. His first important mission was to cross the Appalachian mountains in winter to persuade the French settlers in Canada not to penetrate into the English-speaking colonies. The French reply was negative, but Washington was promoted to colonel for his courage.

In Love — Washington fought for a long time against the French. He fell in love with a young widow and married her. He then resigned from the army and returned to his vast estate.

The Tax On Tea — In the meantime, the British government had demanded new taxes from its colony, causing great discontent. As a gesture of protest against the tax on tea, a number of men disguised as Indians stole on board three British ships in Boston harbor and threw the cargoes of tea into the sea. It was clear that revolution was in the air.

Revolution — The first American congresses were held in Philadelphia in 1774 and 1775. It was during these meetings that the representatives of the thirteen colonies decided to rise against the King's men.

Victory — George Washington was appointed supreme commander of the rebel troops. There followed a long, drawn-out war with Britain. The Americans were defeated on more than one occasion early in the Revolutionary War, but Washington forced his adversaries to surrender at Yorktown in 1781.

His Resignation — The independence of the United States of America was now an established fact. Washington bade farewell to the army by gathering his loyal officers in the Fraunce tavern for a last toast to the new nation. Then he went home to Virginia.

President — The United States had further need for his talents and he was elected President at the first elections to be held under the new Constitution. So Washington came back to serve his fellow countrymen. He held the office of President for eight years. He died in 1799.

Weather Forecasting

Scatterbrains! — These children are quite scatterbrained! They've gone for a picnic in the country and have settled down to sunbathe right under a large, black cloud. Now it's raining. Some children go for a stroll with their umbrellas up or wearing raincoats and boots when there's not a cloud in sight! Really, they are so silly! Why don't they look through the curtains before they leave the house! They should listen to the weather forecast the day before their trip. Then they wouldn't be caught unaware.

The Weather Forecast — Some years ago newspapers and radio did not give the weather forecast. In those far off days people drew on their own experience to judge the weather. They watched nature; they scanned the sky, found out the direction of the wind and saw what the animals were doing. Animals and birds behave in a certain way according to the weather conditions. Country people say that swallows fly low when bad weather is coming and if the frogs croak in the evening, there will be fair weather on the next day.

The Meteorological Office — How do radio and TV announcers know about the weather?

The Meteorological Office keeps in touch with weather stations where scientists observe the sky, the clouds and the winds, and work out the forecast based on their findings.

Weather Stations — All over the world the scientists keep in touch with each other and exchange information about winds, air pressure and cloud build-up. With this information, they can predict rain, sunshine and wind direction. Sometimes, however, the wind suddenly changes its course and the forecast is no longer accurate. In the picture, you can see man-made satellites that transmit high altitude photos to earth with useful data for weathermen.

When It Rains — Let's take an example of weather forecasting. On the 19th of the month it is raining over the sea. The wind is blowing the rain clouds toward the land.

It is almost the 20th and you can forecast that, if the wind does not change, it will be cloudy weather with rain on the 21st.

Plants And The Weather — Plants too can "feel" the weather. When rain is on the way, the ground thistle flower closes its petals, even on a fine day. Daisies do the same.

Rain

Confusion! — It's really hard to get around on a rainy day. People keep poking each other with their umbrellas, cars splash water all over your clothes and you have to watch out for water spouting from leaking drain-pipes overhead.

Floods — Does this mean that rain is always useful? Not really. Too much rain may fall, and the ground cannot drain it off quickly enough, so the streams and rivers begin to swell. They overflow their banks and flood the surrounding area.

A Good Wash — Rain is useful, though, because it washes roofs, balconies and roadways. Like a shower, it washes away all the dust. The air becomes cleaner too. As they fall, the raindrops bring down the specks of dust we breathe into our lungs that hang in the air. After a shower of rain, the air is much fresher, and in summer it is cooler.

In The Countryside — The farmer is delighted to see rain. Now his land and crops will get a refreshing drink.

When It Rains — High up in the sky, all the raindrops hang tightly together in what we see as white clouds. When the clouds come into contact with cold air, the drops of water cling even more closely together, and in doing so become heavier. The air can no longer hold them in the sky and so they fall to earth.

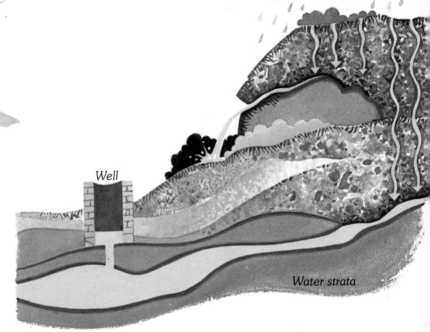

Well

Water strata

What Makes It Rain? — We know that rain comes from the sky and that clouds bring rain. We know that the wind blows the clouds. But what causes clouds to form? If you look at the picture, you will understand. Each day, the sun evaporates moisture from the sea, the ground and the trees. The tiny drops of moisture rise into the sky to form the clouds.

Springs — What would we drink if there were no rain? The rain feeds the springs and the water-bearing layers under the ground. The rainwater drains through the soil and into cracks in the rocks where it collects in natural undergound "tanks".

Underground Caves

Underneath The Mountain — The children's torches light up the cave. The class has come for a guided visit. Isn't it amazing! The garlands of rock all round the walls look like human handiwork, while long, sharp spears shaped like icicles point down from the roof. Water is dripping from their tips. On the ground, exactly below the drips, stand rocky pinnacles. In fact, the wonderful "carvings" inside most caves are made by the action of dripping water.

In The Depths Of The Earth — Far below the rock lie many secret caves, hollowed out by the action of water. Some of them have been discovered by explorers, but many have never been seen because their entrances are so well hidden.

Water Travels — Rainwater drains into the soil and as it sinks, it comes to a crack in the rock. It runs into this crack and, in time, wears away the rock, making a channel. It then runs on until it comes back to the surface again as a sparkling spring.

Snow

A Holiday For The Children — Children are always thrilled when it snows. How pretty the fields, hills, rooftops, trees and bushes look when they're white with snow! And what fun it is to go sledding, go skiing or play in the snow. Even the trees benefit, because the layer of snow protects them from the chill winter wind.

In The Town — It is not easy to get around after a snowfall. The sidewalks are slippery and the snow turns to slush and is splashed all over you by each passing car. When the temperature drops to freezing point the roads are very dangerous for drivers. Snow is much more fun in the country, where it stays undisturbed longer.

Some animal tracks in the snow

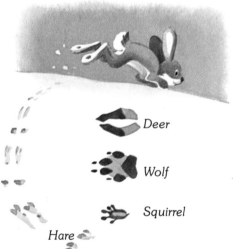

Deer

Wolf

Squirrel

Hare

When Snow Is On The Way — Before rain can turn into snow, the temperature must fall to freezing point. If it is above freezing the raindrops remain liquid. When the temperature is too low, there is no snow. If the sky is clear after a fall of snow, the weather will be cold and you must put on your warmest clothes.

Wild Creatures — Snow makes life difficult for wild creatures because they have nothing to eat. With snow on the ground, there are no berries, seeds or grass to be found. If you visit lonely spots in the country, you'll see the tracks of animals that have come out of their burrows in search of food.

What Is Snow? — If the snowplow did not keep the roads clear, the cars would not be able to pass and many remote villages would be cut off all winter. But what exactly is snow? What is it made of? Snow is rain which is frozen into tiny ice crystals in the sky. If you look at a snowflake under a magnifying glass, you will see that these ice crystals are star-shaped.

Avalanches — You should never linger below a sheer mountain slope after a heavy snowfall. An avalanche might crash down from above, sweeping away everything in its path. Whole mountain villages have been swept away by avalanches and many animals are buried by them in winter.

The Snowplow — The snowplow is a machine which has a pair of large blades to clear away the snow from the roads, piling it by the roadside or spraying it over the sidewalks.

Where There's Always Snow — Some parts of the globe are never free from snow. The regions round the North and South Poles are always covered with snow, so no plants are able to grow there.

Wind

Naughty Wind — It is very windy today and you have to lean into the wind to keep your balance. Autumn leaves are falling and the wind whips them away, whirling them into the air and into people's faces. The wind also raises a cloud of dust that gets into your eyes, and blows hats away as though playing tricks. It slams windows and doors shut. At certain times of the year, mostly in summer, the wind may turn into a hurricane which can blow down crumbling balconies and chimney pots.

Is The Wind Good Or Bad? — We've made the wind sound like a nasty force, but this is not so. When it is not too strong, man can make good use of wind power. It freshens the air and takes away the dirt. It drives the clouds to where rain is needed. It cools the air on hot summer days. And it keeps your kite flying! What more could you want?

Bad Deeds — But when it blows hard, the wind uproots trees, damages crops, and blows birds' nests away. When the trees fall, they may block the entrances to animals' burrows.

Over Sea And Desert — Just imagine what the wind is able to do when there are no hills or buildings to hinder it. It whips up the waves, making passengers on big ships feel sick and overturning small boats. In the desert, it causes sand storms and buries tents and camels under a rain of sand.

Where Does It Come From? — Let's try to solve this mystery. Why does the wind blow? Look at the picture above. When air becomes hot, it also becomes lighter in weight and rises, just as an air-filled balloon drifts upwards. When the hot air rises, cold air takes its place. Cold air is heavy so it falls, causing wind. The blue arrows show the hot air rising, the pink arrow indicates the arrival of cold air.

Wind Is A Worker — Having such a force, wind does a lot of work. Man uses it to turn the sails of his windmills, and to power his yacht. In the desert, it scatters the sand, building dunes and then blowing them away again. It shifts the sand on the seashore too. It even does a spot of modeling. Look at this picture. The wind gave this rock its mushroom shape; it hurled grains of sand against it, until after many years all the soft parts were worn away.

Eastern America

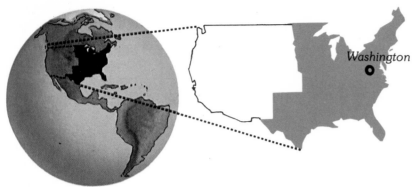

Fifty States — 48 of the 50 states of the United States of America lie at the center of the North American continent; the remaining two are Alaska, at the northern tip of the continent, and Hawaii, a group of islands in the middle of the Pacific Ocean. Most of the east and central states are flat and the only important mountain range is the Appalachians. The plains, especially where the Mississippi river flows, are very fertile. It is here the cowboys round up the herds on the ranches and where cotton, wheat and soy are grown on a vast scale. Florida lies to the south, a peninsula that juts into the sea to form the Gulf of Mexico. Some of the biggest cities in the world stand facing the Atlantic. These eastern states were the first to be colonized by the white settlers.

Presented by France, the Statue of Liberty greets new arrivals from afar. The statue stands in New York harbor.

New York — This is one of America's most important cities. Built at the mouth of the Hudson River, it has about nine million inhabitants, and is particularly famous for its skyscrapers. Here you can see the change in style between St Patrick's Cathedral completed in 1879, and the high-rise buildings which surround it.

St Patrick's Cathedral

Empire State Building

Washington — The capital of the United States was founded less than 200 years ago and is a completely modern city. It has many famous buildings, especially the White House where the president lives, and Capitol Hill, the seat of Congress (illustrated above).

Skyscrapers — The Empire State Building was built in 1931. It towers over New York and is a very popular tourist attraction.

The Bison — In the 1800s the vast prairies were the home of millions of bison. There are practically none left now, and dairy cows and beef herds are raised where once the bison roamed.

Niagara Falls — These famous falls lie on the Canadian border. Though they are not especially long, with a drop of 150 feet (50 meters), the enormous mass of water roars down with a tremendous thundering sound.

The Mississippi — This is one of the longest rivers on earth. Boats can follow its course all the way to the Gulf of Mexico, while its tributaries spread over the central plains of the states. Here is a typical Mississippi riverboat chugging upstream.

The Highways — The United States has more cars than any other country in the world. Cities are linked by multi-lane highways with an efficient system of ring roads and overpasses. The railroads are also highly organized, and extend all over the country.

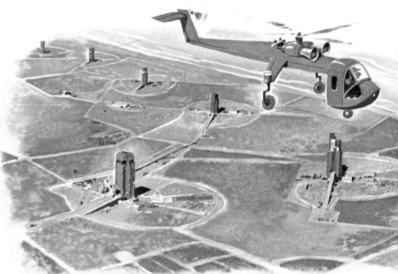

Cape Canaveral — Cape Canaveral, the famous space launching base, is situated in Florida. The first spaceships that went to the moon blasted off from here. This is an aerial view of part of the base.

The Rural Areas — Large areas of the plains have been turned into arable land, where modern farm machinery helps to increase production.

Western America

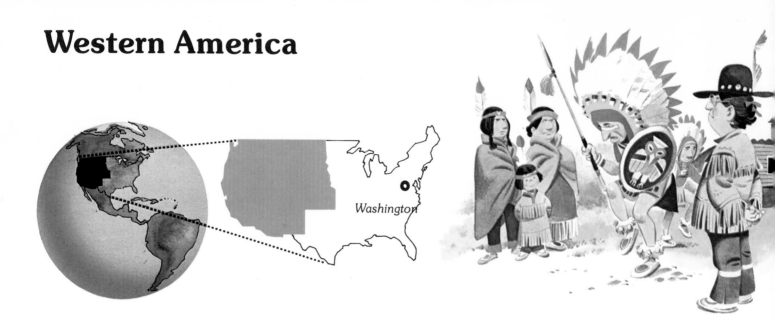

Washington

The "Wild" West — Most of the Western states are mountainous and dry, indeed certain regions are desert. The Rocky Mountains, with peaks over 12,000 feet (4,000 meters) are a barrier to communications to the south between the central plains and the Pacific coast. To the north, the mountains become less harsh and form a vast plateau, but another mountain range, the Sierra Nevadas, stands between these and the ocean. Here the rivers rush down deep narrow gulleys, known as canyons, and millions of years ago, huge lakes lapped the foot of the mountains. These gradually dried up and few remain today, one of them being the well known Salt Lake. The events of the Wild West that we see in films took place in these regions. Here lie the gold, silver and copper mines, and further south, large quantities of oil have been found.

The Native Americans — The Indians were once the owners of all this land. When the white settlers moved in, fierce fighting took place and the Indians were eventually defeated. The remaining tribes now live on Reservations, which are sections of land for their exclusive use. However, the young people generally leave their reservations and head for the towns to find work.

The Pueblos — The south-western Indians, called Pueblos, were not nomads. They tilled the soil and lived in mud brick villages like the one shown above.

The Grand Canyon — This is the greatest of all the American canyons. For millions of years the Colorado River has been flowing between its walls, eating through the rock. At certain spots, the cliffs tower to a height of 6,000 feet (2,000 meters).

The Giants — Giant busts of four great Presidents of the United States — Washington, Lincoln, Jefferson and Roosevelt — stand carved out of the rock face on Mount Rushmore in Dakota.

Yellowstone — This is one of America's most famous national parks. It extends over a huge stretch of mountainous country and is the home of many species of wildlife. This is the home of a favorite cartoon character, Yogi Bear.

Los Angeles — This is the biggest city on the Pacific coast. It is well known for its airplane industry, and its fame to nearby Hollywood. Los Angeles sprawls for many miles and the various sectors of the city are linked by a web of freeways.

The Desert — Much of Arizona is desert and the very scanty plant life consists of shrubs and thorny succulents like these giant candelabra cacti.

Rodeos — A traditional western show is the rodeo. In one competition, the rider has to tame unbroken horses, just as the old pioneers did in the last century.

The Geysers — One of the finest sights in Yellowstone is the hot geysers. They are volcanic in origin and regularly spout jets of boiling water into the air. The biggest jet spouts every hour and reaches a height of 150 feet (50 meters).

Canada

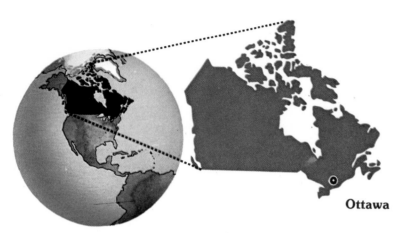

Ottawa

Lakes And Forests — Canada is the second largest country in the world. It is found on the map just north of the United States of America, on the continent of North America. Half its territory is forest, most of it still untouched by man. Lakes are dotted all over Canada, some very large. To the south, the climate is mild and wheat is a major crop. In the north, the coastline becomes rugged and barren. It is split into a series of islands that reach the Arctic Circle and are frozen over for most of the year. Toward the Pacific Ocean, the land is all mountains, where the Rocky Mountains continue together with other high ranges. From these heights the great Canadian rivers flow down to meet the Arctic seas. Canada has a small population and a wealth of natural resources, which have not yet been fully exploited. The country is crossed by 50,000 miles (70,000 kilometers) of railroad and more than 650,000 miles (800,000 kilometers) of roads. The two languages spoken are English and French. Ottawa is the capital.

Boys wearing ice hockey gear; hockey is Canada's national sport

The Totems — Many Indians used to inhabit Canada, and some still live in their own villages. Here are several totem poles, tree trunks carved to represent Indian gods.

Central Canada — The center of Canada is dotted with lakes, and there are thousands of them all over the country, some as big as inland seas. Here is a typical view of the countryside.

Wheat — The most modern kinds of machinery are used in the cultivation of wheat on the prairies. Canada produces more than she could ever use and a lot is exported to other countries.

The Mounties — The Royal Canadian Mounted Police have been featured in many films and stories, though they don't ride on horses so much nowadays. The Mounted Police use cars and motorcycles like other police forces.

Farther north, winters are longer and colder. This is a typical Yukon scene, where the temperature can fall to −80° in winter.

The Guards — Many traditions have been handed down from the time when most of Canada was a British colony. In the picture, you can see the changing of the guard in front of Parliament in Ottawa; this ceremony is similar to the one held at Buckingham Palace in England.

Frontenac Castle

Quebec — This is the chief French-speaking city, on the banks of the St Lawrence River. In the picture is Frontenac Castle which dominates the old town.

Ottawa — The capital of Canada has roughly 500,000 inhabitants, and therefore is not the biggest city. For example, other cities like Montreal have over two million inhabitants.

The Beavers — Various kinds of animal live in the Canadian woods. The best known is the beaver, builder of underwater colonies and dams across mountain streams.

Mexico

The Plateau — Mexico is a hot and mostly dry country. It is situated south of the United States, where North America narrows into a corridor of land. To the west is the Pacific Ocean; the Atlantic on the east forms the Gulf of Mexico. Two mountain ranges, both called the Sierras, lie a short distance from the coast and form the edges of the central plateau. This plateau was once without any vegetation but now is covered with flourishing cotton plantations thanks to irrigation schemes. Toward the south, the plateau ends in a series of volcanic peaks over 5,000 feet (1,700 meters) high. Here, in the hottest and wettest part of the country, stands the capital, Mexico City. Luxuriant, tropical vegetation is found here, with great forests and cocoa, coffee and sugar cane plantations. Some of the oldest American civilizations originated here, and many Mexicans are descended from ancient peoples such as the Maya.

The Maya — Here are some of the Mayan remains to be found in Mexico. Later, the Maya spread into Central America as well. They put up a terrific struggle against the Spanish invaders, but in the end their beautiful cities were destroyed.

The Yucca — These strange plants with tufts of leaves at the tip of each branch are yuccas, typical of the plants to be found in the arid plateaux of the interior.

Cactus And Agave — Here are two other kinds of plant typical of the waterless parts of northern Mexico. A tough fiber called sisal is obtained from the pulpy leaves of the agave, which is used for making rough cloth. Tequila, a very alcoholic drink is distilled from the pulp of the same plant.

Cactus

Yucca

Agave

The Churches — Many baroque churches exist as reminders of the Spanish conquest. In the picture is Mexico City Cathedral, which was partly built in the baroque style.

Mexico City — Mexico City stands at a height of 15,631 feet (2,277 meters) on the site of the ancient capital of the Aztecs, another ancient people. It has around eight million inhabitants. Some of the buildings on the campus of the University of Mexico are shown in the picture.

The Fishermen — The highlands are dotted with lakes full of fish. The fishermen go out in small boats and use oval-shaped nets like those shown in the picture.

The Sombrero — Most village people wear a sombrero in the extremely hot Mexican climate. Its wide brim shades the face from the sun.

Feast Days — The Mexicans love holidays. Each religious feast day is a good reason to hold processions and dances in traditional costumes and to enjoy the music of the local band.

The Toltecs — The origins of this ancient people who once inhabited Mexico are still not clearly known. These carved pillars were once part of a Toltec temple, long since vanished.

The Pacific Ocean

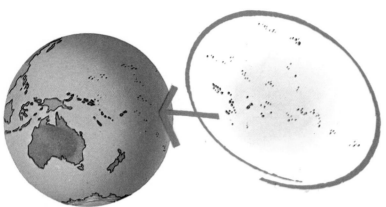

In The Pacific — Oceania is made up of hundreds of islands, large and small. Polynesia is the group of islands farthest to the east, separated from the American coast by the Pacific Ocean. These islands are either volcanic in origin or formed by coral. They are surrounded by warm seas and enjoy a very mild climate. Many of them are covered with palm groves, ensuring a good supply of coconuts. Small communities of fishermen live on some of the islands, but many are uninhabited. Important towns are only found on the larger islands, where agriculture is better developed. World-famous islands such as Hawaii and Eastern Samoa, which are part of the United States, and Easter Island which belongs to Chile, are all in Polynesia. The first European to land on the Polynesian islands was Ferdinand Magellan, in about 1500, but they were explored fully only recently.

The Rock — Many of these islands are made of coral. They are fomed when the shells of millions upon millions of the tiny corals build up to make a solid mass.

Coral | Coral
Submerged mountain

Coral — All the shallow seas of Polynesia are lined with beautiful branching coral. Though they look like the twigs from some strange plant, they are really the shells of tiny polyps that wave their tiny tentacles out of the holes in search of something to eat. The corals grow on top of each other in a colony, forming crusts many feet thick.

Atolls — When the coral colonies grow around the cone of an underwater mountain, they form a ring. If the coralline deposits become so great that they emerge from the ocean, the resulting island will be circular too. These little coral islands are called atolls and are dotted all over the ocean.

The Hawaiian Islands — Every tourist knows of these islands, and hordes of visitors come to them to see the ceremonial dances and the flower festivals.

Boats — The Polynesians are fine sailors who regularly cross the wide straits from one island to the next. They use outrigger canoes like this one, which are very seaworthy.

Mats — Beautiful mats are woven from palm leaves and are used for floor coverings and curtain material. Matting is also used instead of bricks for walls and for making shelters.

Fishing — The staple food of the Polynesian islanders is fish. The islanders are excellent fishermen, but they often run into danger from the sharks which infest these seas.

The Statues Of Easter Island — Easter Island is world famous for its mysterious giant stone heads. They were carved by a race of people that has long since vanished.

EUROPE

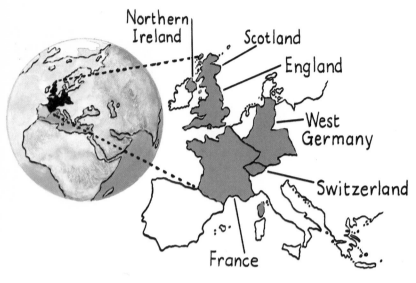

Big Ben   *Westminster Cathedral*

London — Visitors to London like to see the famous monuments such as Big Ben, the clock at the Palace of Westminster. Westminster Cathedral is another famous landmark.

Great Britain

Tower Bridge — London is built on both sides of the River Thames. One bridge which spans the Thames is Tower Bridge. The lower section opens to let big ships pass through. The upper section is a gangway 155 feet (47 meters) high which joins the two towers.

France

Tradition — Great Britain is a land of tradition. One is the Changing of the Guard, a military exercise carried out in front of Buckingham Palace, where the Royal family lives.

The Bagpipes — The traditional Scottish costume is the tartan kilt, which is still worn on ceremonial occasions. Bagpipes are well known throughout the world for the unique sound they produce.

The Wine — French vineyards are famous throughout the world. France also produces many different types of cheese which it exports all over Europe.

Industry — Germany has rich resources of coal and iron ore. Its steel industry employs over 100,000 people. Other major industries include car production, chemicals and machinery plants.

German cars are famous throughout the world

Paris — The Eiffel Tower was built for the Exposition of 1899. Many artists make their home in the city, for Paris is considered an important center of art.

West Germany

Brandenburg Gate

The Heart Of Europe — Surrounded by a number of other countries, Germany lies at the heart of Europe. It also has a seaboard along which have been built large and important ports.

Berlin — This magnificent city was almost destroyed during World War II and has since been rebuilt in an ultra-modern style. A famous monument is the Brandenburg Gate (above) which was built after the war.

Switzerland

Alpine Horns — Switzerland is a mountainous country. The shepherds used to use long horns made of pine wood to call from one valley to the next. These horns are still a feature of local festivals.

Chalets — A well known sight is the chalet, built of wood with a slate roof. Switzerland is famous for its fine clocks and watches. Cheese and chocolate are two traditional Swiss products.

97

EUROPE

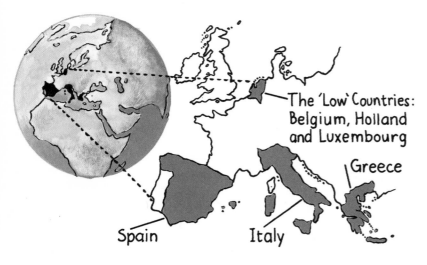

The 'Low' Countries: Belgium, Holland and Luxembourg

Greece

Spain   Italy

Italy

The Boot — Italy is shaped like a giant boot. There is a mountain range in the north and another running down the middle. Much of this rock can be cut into the marble blocks for which Italy is famous. Rome is the capital of Italy and has some fascinating ruins from the time of Ancient Rome, including Senate Hill and the Colosseum. Vatican City, where the Pope lives, is an independent state within Rome itself. There are many excellent museums and art galleries in Italy.

The Low Countries

Windmills — Windmills are a common sight in Belgium, Holland and Luxembourg, the three nations that make up the Low Countries. They are called this because the land is often at a lower level than the sea. Dykes hold back the water from the land.

Tulips — Whole stretches of land are used to grow tulips. Nearly all the bulbs are sold abroad. Dutch tulips are famous all over the world.

Venice — This famous city is built on a series of islands. There are no cars because there are no streets. Gondolas that travel up and down are the only form of transportation.

Palazzo Vecchio   *Milan Duomo*

Leaning Tower of Pisa

Giotto's Campanile   *Campanile of Siena Duomo*

Famous Buildings — Italy has hundreds of famous buildings and monuments. Above you can see some of the most well known.

Greece

The Acropolis — The Ancient Greeks were a very advanced people. The Acropolis was the heart of the ancient city of Athens. Many temples and important buildings still remain.

Thermopylae — The Greeks were a brave people who fought fiercely against their enemies. The picture shows a monument to soldiers who died to prevent the Persians from invading in 480 B.C.

Industry — Sponge fishing is a flourishing industry in Greece. Another is grape growing. Most Greek grapes are dried to produce raisins.

Spain

The Flamenco — Tourists come to Spain for the sunshine, beaches, art galleries and the traditional dances and costumes. The flamenco is the best known Spanish dance.

The Cuevas — Cuevas are homes dug out of hillsides. A very ancient people prefer to live there rather than in towns. The ancestors of these people may have been the ones who did the famous rock paintings of Altamira.

The Hinny — Spain is still mainly an agricultural country. Here is the hinny which is a cross-breed from a horse and a donkey and, like a mule, is used to carry loads and helps on the farm.

American Deserts

Plant Life — It is not true that there's no life at all in the desert. In American deserts there are huge spiny cactus plants that survive the dryness and flower after a rare shower of rain moistens the earth. Little clumps of verbena and bright petunias peep up from the sand. Many creatures live there, too: rodents, insects, snakes, and even quite large animals such as the lynx and the puma.

Jack rabbit

Ground squirrel

Kangaroo rat

Rodents — Here are some of the desert rodents. They come out of their holes at night when the air is cool in search of seeds and berries. One member of the family acts as a guard, ready to give the alarm at the first sign of danger.

Chipmunk

Cotton mouse

The Coyote — The howl of the coyote rings nightly among the rocky outcrops as he calls his fellows to the hunt.

The coyote resembles the wolf, but its gray coat is softer and thicker. It leaves the prairie and hunts over barren ground in search of food. Coyotes almost always hunt in packs and surround the victim in order to cut off its escape. One of their favorite prey is the pronghorn antelope.

Puma

The Big Cats — Here are the puma and the lynx, feared by all the other inhabitants of the desert. They are ferocious and strong, but not as big as their relations who live in the jungle and savannah.

Lynx

Pronghorn antelope

The Rattlesnake — This snake is fairly common in the desert. Its skin is the same color as the stones in which it lies waiting for its prey. The rattler's bite is poisonous to animals and people. It gets its name from the "rattle" on the end of its tail. This is really a set of horny rings which click together and sound like castanets when the angry snake shakes its tail. Sometimes, when this warning sound is heard, there is still time to escape.

Under The Stones — Many of the small desert creatures make their homes under stones where it is cool and the soil is damp. Some of these are poisonous and they hunt other little creatures for food.

Tarantula

Scorpion

101

The Arctic

Among The Icy Wastes — The North Pole is a deserted land swept by icy gales, where vast areas of snow and ice stretch as far as the eye can see. As in the desert, however, only a few animals find enough food to survive. Not all of them are tiny creatures either. Walrus and polar bears are big and heavy, and some of the seals are large. Many kinds of fish live underneath the ice. The Arctic fox, wolves and large birds of prey venture into this frozen land to hunt small mammals. Since the beginning of history, a hardy race of people has learnt how to live in these snowy wastes. They are the Eskimoes, the people who used to live in igloos. Igloos are houses built out of blocks of frozen snow placed on top of each other.

The Polar Bear — This animal may weigh up to 990 lbs (450 kilos) and its thick white fur makes it look even larger. The polar bear's favorite meal is a tasty seal, but it is quite happy to catch fish, sea otters or any other animal. It blends in so well with the white background that its victims do not notice it.

The Walrus — The walrus may look rather ferocious with its long tusks, but it is really the most peaceful of animals. It spends most of its time sleeping on the ice and dives into the sea only to nose around the bottom in search of shellfish for a meal. A neighbor of this kindly giant is the sea lion, which is really a seal. It gets its name from the lion-like mane on the back of its neck.

The Seals — Seals are about the nicest animals you could meet! They look clumsy as they drag themselves across the ice shelf on their flippers but once in the water they are transformed into agile and expert swimmers. They are the best fishers in the sea and will never go hungry as long as there are fish around. Often, they hunt underneath the surface of the ice and break breathing holes in the icy crust so that they can pop up for a breath of fresh air. The Eskimo hunters wait for them at these holes and catch the seals as they bob up. Below you can see the cod, a common fish of northern waters.

The Narwhal — Another inhabitant of the northern seas is the narwhal, a large creature with a long spear on its snout. It is not a fish, as you might expect, but a mammal like a dolphin or whale. Its spear is simply a canine tooth that, for some strange reason, has developed right out of the narwhal's mouth, twisting as it grows.

Below you can see a puffin, easily recognized by its thick, bright-colored beak. It spends its time fishing.

Puffin

Guillemot

Narwhal

Cod

103

The Antarctic

The Sixth Continent — The vast sheet of ice that surrounds the South Pole is quite different from that at the North Pole. The South Pole is colder and completely different species of animals live there. A buried continent lies underneath the ice, rich in minerals and metals which man may find a use for one day. Explorers have drilled underneath the ice cap and found fossil coal. This shows that, a long time ago, the land was not covered with ice but by great forests. The mystery of what happened to this continent has yet to be solved.

The Leopard Seal — Seals who live in the south are different from those that live in the Arctic. The favorite food of the ferocious leopard seal is a tasty penguin.

The Killer Whale — Another dangerous animal which lives in the southern seas is the killer whale. This gigantic mammal often grows up to 27 feet (9 meters) long.

Penguins — Penguins live in huge colonies on the ice cap. They cannot fly but are marvelous swimmers and can stay under the water for quite a long time.

Tuxedoes — With their black and white plumage and erect strutting walk, penguins look like little men in tuxedoes. Their height varies from about 18 inches to just over 3 feet (½−1 meter).

Great skua

Antarctic pigeon

Long-tailed skua

The Sea Elephant — This good-natured giant of the South Pole is quite plump! It can grow to a length of 18 feet (6 meters) and can weigh a couple of tons. It lies in the sun all day and only enters the water to find food for supper.

Shrimp — Fish and shrimp are the main sources of food for most of the birds and animals that live at the South Pole. The sea round the ice cap is rich in both and it has been calculated that about 30,000 shrimp live in one square yard of water!

105

The Race To The Poles

The White Desert — The polar regions were one of the last places on earth to be explored. An expedition to these areas needed careful planning, complete knowledge of the effects of cold and suitable means for living any length of time in the icy wastes. The early explorers who ventured into the northern territories tried to imitate the way the Eskimoes lived but their expeditions were often a failure because white men were not trained to endure the severe conditions of a polar winter. It was at the beginning of this century that the two famous explorers, F. A. Cook and Robert Peary, succeeded in reaching the North Pole. Both expeditions used sleds pulled by husky teams. Not long before, a Norwegian called Fridtjof Nansen had come close to the Pole after an exhausting journey by ship and then on foot. Three years after the conquest of the North Pole, the South Pole was reached too. The first expedition to arrive was led by Roald Amundsen, a Norwegian. He beat the Briton, Robert Falcon Scott by some weeks. Scott's party reached the Pole on 17 January, 1912. Scott perished with his companions on the return journey. Today, aircraft and helicopters make it much easier to reach the Poles and each year scientific expeditions visit these regions, especially the Antarctic icefields under which lies an entire continent.

The Pioneers — One of the first men to explore the North Pole was a Dutchman called Barents. This is a reproduction of the cabin in which he spent the winter at New Zemlja, in 1596.

Nansen — Nansen's ship was held fast in the ice as the Norwegian tried to reach the North Pole in 1893. He continued on foot but had to give up and make his way back in an Eskimo kayak during the thaw.

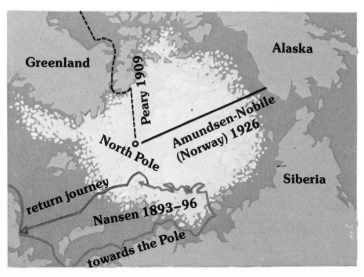

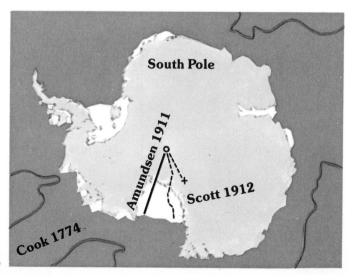

Cook and Peary — After unbelievable hazards and troubles, expeditions led by F. A. Cook and Robert Peary reached the North Pole for the first time in 1909.

The Antarctic — A famous explorer called Captain Cook sailed right around the Antarctic Circle in 1773 and discovered a number of islands. He did not touch the continent that lies under the South Pole.

By Air — Some time later, Amundsen and Nobile flew over the North Pole. Nobile then attempted to repeat this feat but his craft crashed and most of his men lost their lives. The survivors waited to be rescued inside a red tent on the ice.

Below The Icecap — In 1958 the American atomic submarine Nautilus passed under the Arctic icecap and reached the North Pole.

Ross — The first man to set foot on this continent was the explorer, James Clark Ross, who landed at a point where great icy walls rose out of the sea. This was in 1840. Today this place is called the Ross Ice Shelf.

Amundsen — Roald Amundsen, who had acquired great experience of the Northern icy wastes, was the first man to reach the South Pole in December 1911. A few days later, Scott also reach the Pole but unfortunately died on the return journey.

107

Glaciers And Ice

A River Of Ice — This little boy and his father have climbed a mountain. Now they're admiring the sight of the great glacier descending from a faraway peak like a river of ice. Some parts of the earth are icebound all the year round, even in places where the climate is quite warm. Glaciers lie among the peaks of many of the world's mountains.

A Moving River — Glaciers are rivers of ice. They appear to lie motionless but are really moving very, very slowly down the mountainside. As they move, they carry dirt and rocks along with them.

Crevasses — A glacier is not one huge solid block of moving ice. Large pieces break off, leaving deep cracks called crevasses. It is dangerous to cross a glacier without a guide and the right equipment.

How A Glacier Is Formed — Where does all the ice come from? How did it get there? The answer is quite simple: from the snow. When it snows heavily on mountain peaks where it is always cold, the thick layers of snow never have a chance to melt. As time passes, this snow is pressed down by fresh layers and turns into ice.

The Father Of Rivers — People say that a glacier is the father of a river. This is true, for the stream that emerges from beneath the ice flows on downhill gathering momentum as it goes.

The Great Glaciers — The greatest glaciers in the world are those around the North and South Poles. These immense sheets of ice are as big as whole countries, stretching down to the edge of the sea. The ice cap at the South Pole is more than a mile (2 kilometers) thick in places. As the ice moves, the edges are pushed into the sea where they break off and create icebergs.

The Foot Of A Glacier — The glacier moves over the rocky surface until it reaches the valley floor. Heat from the soil causes it to melt. A trickle of water flows under the glacier, becoming a stream that tunnels its way under the ice. By the time it emerges into daylight, it is a rushing torrent.

The Steppes

Kingdom Of The Winds — In Eastern Europe and parts of Russia there are open stretches of plain, called steppes. The climate is always cold there and icy winds make life hard for the animals and plants. The steppes are thinly covered with short grass that barely grows, and low stunted trees. The rains fall once a year, and only then do little tufts of new grass sprout and the steppes turn green. Wild goats and other herbivores (grass-eaters) graze delightedly, because the rest of the year their only food is the scant dry vegetation that remains. Predators are found on the steppes, some of them quite large, such as the wild cats, bears and wolves. They prey on the grass-eaters and birds.

The Camel — This domestic animal is the nomadic tribespeople's most faithful friend. The camel can travel over the desolate wastelands for days on end in all weathers, without a drop of water or a mouthful of food. Its thick coat gives a warm wool and its milk is very nourishing. Anyone who lives in the steppes must own a camel.

The Wild Cat — Many of the birds in this area nest on the ground, because of the shortage of trees. They do not have an easy life, however, for the prowling wild cat is their greatest enemy. Though fairly small, the wild cat is as fierce as any tiger.

The Wild Goat — The goat has had no difficulty in adapting to the harsh conditions of life on these windy plains. Goats will eat the roughest kind of food, even the dried grass that covers the steppes most of the year. The tender buds that goats most enjoy sprout only after the rains. The wild goat sometimes wanders as far as the mountains and climbs up to the high ridges.

Tamarisk

Wild rhubarb

Mugwort

The Tents — The nomads' tents are round and made from skins. When the nomads move on in search of richer grazing for their flocks, they pack their homes on to the camels.

Jumping rat

Rabbit

Hamster

Jerboa

The Saiga Antelope — Certain species of antelope manage to survive on the steppes even though food is scarce. Herds of saiga cover great distances every day in search of food.

The Rodents — Large numbers of rodents live on the steppes, usually in burrows. They come out mostly at night to feed on grass, bits of bark and whatever seeds they can find.

111

The Savannah

A Sea Of Grass — Between the African jungle and the desert lies an immense plain of tall grass, broken here and there by clumps of low trees. This is the savannah, a sea of green grass in spring that turns yellow in summer. It is the home of a very large number of grass-eating and flesh-eating animals.

The Hunt — The huge quantities of food available in the savannah attract large numbers of grass-eating animals, such as various species of gazelle, zebras, giraffes and elephants. These grass-eaters in their turn attract the carnivorous (flesh-eating) animals. The flesh-eaters lie in wait in the savannah and at the waterholes to leap out on any unwary creature. Lions and other fierce beasts make their home in clumps of trees and rocky outcrops. The remains of their meals are swiftly cleaned up by scavengers, such as hyenas and vultures.

The Cheetah — Most of the flesh-eating animals lie in wait for their prey near the waterholes and then leap out. But the cheetah chases its prey across the savannah, often for a great distance. The cheetah is swifter than any gazelle or fleeing zebra.

The Baobab — Odd trees grow in the savannah. One of these is the huge, stumpy-trunked baobab. It is not much use as timber, however, as its wood is spongy.

The Acacia — Many of the trees that grow in clumps on the savannah are acacias. They are the main source of food for the giraffes, which can reach the leaves easily with their long necks.

The Elephant — Herds of elephants graze on the edge of the savannah. The earth shakes and the monkeys take refuge in the trees when these herds are on the move.

Tropical Rain Forests Of The Amazon

An Adventure — What a wonderful adventure it would be to explore the untamed rain forest! Anyone who has ventured into its depths has been overwhelmed by its wonders. There is no other place on earth where the vegetation is so thick and varied. The treetops seem to touch the sky and their thick foliage and branches shut out all the light. Not a ray of sunlight can penetrate the tangle of branches, and the lower-growing plants and undergrowth are always in shade. The ground is covered with creepers and clusters of highly-scented flowers, while straggling lianas cling to the trees. Parrots and gaily-colored toucans flap about high in the topmost branches, and giant butterflies flit among the leaves. The treetops are the home of the monkeys, very noisy inhabitants of the forest. The jungle and rain forest near the Amazon River in South America is, however, full of danger — there are many huge snakes, as well as the marauding jaguar.

The Jaguar — This is the biggest and most ferocious of the Amazonian cats. It stretches out on a branch overhanging the river, from which it leaps on its prey.

A Wall Of Green — Plants grow and twist so thickly that they form a living wall, which has to be hacked down using a very sharp knife called a machete.

114

Orchids — Look at the exotic flowers that bloom in the rain forest. Orchids do not blossom on the ground but cling to high branches where the sun can reach them.

Macaw

Hummingbird

Parrot

Toucan

The Rubber Tree — The bark of this tree is slit open so the sticky liquid inside can be collected. This is latex which is used to make the rubber that goes into so many everyday articles.

Macaque monkey

Capuchin monkey

White-tufted marmoset

Other Inhabitants — Birds and monkeys are the most common of all the inhabitants of the rain forest. They make their home in the branches and are generally very noisy. The most striking birds are the big parrots, and the toucans with the huge, strangely-shaped beaks. The monkeys swing through the branches on their long arms and often hang by their tails. Below you can see the anaconda, the biggest snake in the world.

Anaconda

The Jungle

Buried Palaces — In the Asian jungle there are whole cities and splendid palaces inhabited only by the monkeys. One of these is the abandoned city of Angkor, once the capital of the kingdom of Khmer. It is now so overrun with plants and vegetation that the roots of giant trees twine round its palace walls. It is very hot and wet in the jungle so the vegetation grows quickly, covering everything in its path. It is not easy to find one's way through the jungle. Many animals and birds live there, and glorious flowers bloom. The treetops are home for hordes of monkeys, and birds of all kinds roost in the branches.

The Tiger — This is the most terrible of the jungle beasts. It is not afraid of any other animal and will kill without the slightest hesitation. When a tiger grows too old and clumsy to hunt its prey, it may creep close to a village and carry off domestic animals. It is just as dangerous as the cobra you can see below.

The Elephant — The Asian elephant lives on the edge of the jungle. It is smaller than its African cousin and is also more docile. The Asian elephant can be tamed and helps man to drag heavy loads or carries him out to the hunt.

116

Bamboo — Bamboo is quite common in the jungle. The tree grows quickly and its slender trunk may reach a height of 120 feet (40 meters). The natives use bamboo to build their houses and eat its shoots as a vegetable.

The Rafflesia Flower — The petals of this enormous flower are big and spongy. Each petal is about 1 foot (30 cm) and a reddish-purple color. The flower weighs several pounds (kgs). They bloom for only a few days.

Quicksands — It can be very dangerous to cross the jungle, and not only because of the snakes and tigers which may attack. In swampy places there are dreadful quicksands, stretches of thick mud that swallow up anyone who steps onto them.

Reptiles — The only clear routes through the jungle are rivers, but it can be risky traveling by boat. Crocodiles live in the rivers and snakes reach down from overhanging branches.

117

The Australian Bush

The Land Of Marsupials — The Australian bush is the home of some of the strangest animals on earth. Here you'll find kangaroos, koala bears and many other mammals that rear their young in a soft furry pouch on their bellies. This is the country where there are some wingless birds whose feathers look like fur coats. Here too lives the duckbilled platypus, a mammal with a beak like a duck's, as well as the anteater that lays eggs. In open country you will see high mud towers. These are termite hills, built by termites to protect and ventilate their underground cities.

Bottle tree

Termite hill

Curious Trees — Many of the trees are shaped very strangely. The bottle tree has a thick, bottle-shaped trunk and the grass tree has a tuft growing out at the top.

Rabbits — The commonest of all mammals in Australia is the wild rabbit, brought over by the first European settlers. It has multiplied and spread to such an extent that it has become a dreadful pest which destroys entire crops.

The Kangaroo — This is the most famous of all Australian animals. The baby kangaroo, or joey, is reared in its mother's pouch. When the kangaroo wants a rest it leans back on the base of its tail. A kangaroo bounds away the minute it senses danger, jumping 6 feet (2 meters) at a time.

Koala

Cockatoo

Count Raggi's bird of paradise

In The Treetops — The eucalyptus is the best known and most typical of all Australian trees. In its branches you will see the koala bears, cuddly-looking animals which were the original teddy bears. Perhaps you will also see some birds, brightly-colored parrots, the lyre bird and the Bird of Paradise, so-called because of its gorgeous plumage. On the ground, you will meet the emu, a large running bird that looks vaguely like the African ostrich. The duckbilled platypus lives in the water. This weird animal has a duck's bill, webbed feet and lays eggs like a bird but feeds its young on its own milk and keeps them in a pouch like a kangaroo.

King of Saxony's bird of paradise

Emu

Eucalyptus

Coral Reefs

Among The Coral — The ocean bed is always a beautiful sight, but the wonderful "flower gardens" that exist in warm waters are like fairyland. These are found along a line of reefs and small islands, where mother-of-pearl and coral colonies have grown so high that they form a long barrier which almost breaks the surface of the water. These coral reefs are the home of hosts of brilliantly-colored fish and millions of beautiful shellfish. Sometimes the coral is deposited all round the peak of an underwater mountain, and grows until it is above the surface of the waves.

Branches Of Stone — Here are some pink corals. They look like flowering branches, yet they are the skeletons of a colony of little star-shaped creatures. Each "flower" that grows out of the branch is a tiny tentacled creature which waves its long arms in search of food. When the creature is frightened it draws in its tentacles and only reappears when it feels safe again.

Sea slug

Hermit crab

Murex

Cone

The Ray — Among the coral reefs live the rays, large flat fish that flap their fins, rather like a bird, when they move. Some species have a poisonous sting.

The Atoll — Here is a little round island made by the deposits of coral and mother-of-pearl. It takes many years to form such an island. In the course of time, the wind carries sand and seeds and then palm trees and other plants grow.

Turtles — The biggest marine turtles in the world are found in the sea around the coral islands. Many of the baby turtles are eaten by preying sea birds and fish but a fully-grown turtle has few real enemies. Its shell is so hard that practically nothing can break it.

The Dugong — Warm seas are the home of many dangerous predators such as sharks, but quite harmless creatures like the dugong also live there. This marine animal lives on nothing but seaweed. Sailors used to mistake it for a human being and that is how the legend of the mermaid began. Unfortunately, the dugong is now almost extinct.

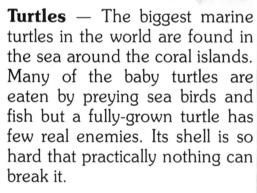

Shark

Dugong

Coal And Its Uses

The Coal Merchant's Yard — Every large town has a coal merchant, who sells coal, logs, and sawdust. Before the development of central heating, and when methane gas, oil and gasoline were not often used, the coal merchant's yard was an important place. In those days, people burned coal and logs to warm their houses. Before electricity and oil fuels were available coal was also used to drive machines in the factories.

Coal For Energy — Only a few years ago, coal was one of the few natural sources of energy that man knew how to utilize. When it burns, coal gives out heat which provides the energy to drive machines. Trains were once pulled by a steam locomotive that left a trail of smoke behind as it puffed along. The coal was shoveled into the bunker, and as it burned it heated the water, making steam that drove the pistons and wheels. Steamships were powered in the same way.

In The Factories — Coal is still used to provide energy in some factories. Blast furnaces burn coal to smelt metals and separate them from the rock and earth in which they are embedded. Many materials are derived from coal, such as perfumes and plastics. Coal is, however, used mostly in the chemical industry. Engineering companies prefer to use electricity and oil, which are more easily connected to the machinery.

In Old Houses — Coal stoves are used in some houses because they give plenty of heat. Many people prefer kerosene stoves and heaters. Kerosene is a by-product of oil and is cleaner and more practical. Many coal stoves are now being installed in new houses because they are cheap to run.

How Coal Is Formed — Coal is all that remains of great forests that fell millions of years ago and were buried in earth and mud. When the layers of mud turned into rock, the wood became coal instead of rotting. Some coal is very ancient, some is of more recent origin, but all of it is very old.

Where It Comes From — Coal lies under the surface of the earth, in seams separated from each other by layers of rock. These coal seams may be far underground. The coal has to be mined and brought up to the surface.

Iron And Its Uses

When Iron Was Unknown — Before 800 B.C. man did not know of the existence of iron, the metal from which so many articles are made today. Primitive man had only stone weapons with which to defend himself from wild beasts or his enemies.

There's Iron Everywhere — Look around wherever you are, in your home or outside. You'll find iron goods everywhere, including familiar things like scissors and kitchen knives, some toys and a host of other things.

Mines — Iron ore may lie under the ground, but the richest deposits lie on the surface.

Blast Furnaces — Pure iron is extracted from the ore in a blast furnace. The furnace is heated to a tremendously high temperature until the ore becomes liquid. It is then poured into molds and allowed to cool. The end product is cast iron, a raw material used in many other processes.

Where Iron Is Found — In its natural state, iron is mixed up with other minerals, and is found either on the earth's surface or under the ground.

Rust — Iron becomes rusty if it is left outside. A coat of anti-rust paint is applied to prevent this.

Ships And Bridges — Here are some more things made of iron: cars, buses, traffic lights, billboards, shutters, trams and tram rails, as well as all sorts of machines. Skyscrapers and suspension bridges may be built of iron and steel. Yet if men had not discovered how to smelt iron, it would all still be ore inside the rock and of no use to anyone. Instead, thousands and thousands of people all over the world are employed in mining and smelting iron and manufacturing many different products with it.

Steel — Steel is obtained by refining iron. Steel is much stronger and more elastic, and so the machinery used in factories is all made of steel. A special steel, called stainless steel, is rust-proof so it never loses its shiny look. Forks, knives, pots and pans are made of stainless steel.

125

Oil — Where It Comes From

gasoline open

Gasoline — We've stopped at a service station to fill the car with gasoline. Gasoline is expensive! "Why does the gasoline cost so much?" someone asks. "Because the price of oil has gone up and so have the taxes!" comes the reply. Now what has oil to do with gasoline? We shall soon find out.

The Refinery — Let's follow the truck that has just emptied its load into the underground tanks at the service station. It is now returning to the refinery, the place where gasoline is obtained from oil. What a maze of pipes and towers there is in an oil refinery!

Oil Tankers — Many countries have no natural sources of oil. So oil is brought to them from oil-producing countries in huge ships called tankers. It is not really correct to speak of "oil-producing countries" for oil is not "produced" in the sense of being manufactured but is pumped up out of the ground. It was formed millions of years ago, before man ever walked the earth.

Oil Wells — The oil is pumped up by wells sunk in the ground. Special drills slice through the hardest rock and deep wells can be dug out. The crude oil is then channeled into huge pipelines that carry it to the seaports.

Oil wells are often worked in the middle of the desert. They are also drilled on the ocean bed from floating platforms called rigs. Work on an oil rig is very hard and sometimes dangerous.

How Oil Is Formed — Of course, you can't just drill a hole in the ground and find oil. Why is oil found in some places and not in others? The presence of oil in a certain part of the world depends on what happened there millions of years ago. In those remote times, large quantities of mud, together with the plants and tiny creatures that lived in it, were trapped between layers of rock. As time passed, it turned into oil. Oil is the result of the transformation of the remains of living things. It can be found either near the earth's surface or at a great depth underground.

Products From Oil — Gasoline is obtained from oil, but so are diesel fuel, naphtha, lubricating oils, paraffin, tar, and many plastic materials.

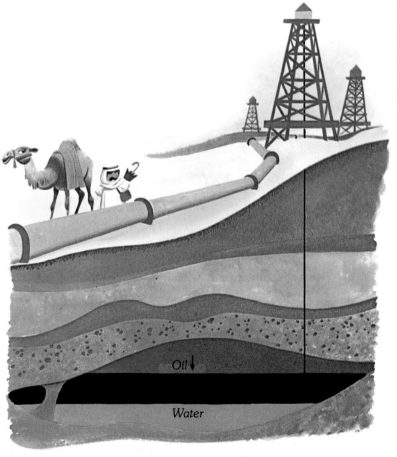

Oil

Water

The Wonder Of Electricity

Sparks — Have you ever stroked a cat's fur and felt it crackle and stand up under your fingers? As you stroked, a most amazing thing happened. You made electricity, and it crackled as it discharged through your hand. Don't you believe this? Well, rub the tip of a plastic ruler with a piece of wool fabric. Pull the curtains or turn off the light and hold your knuckle to the ruler, and you'll see a spark between your knuckle and the ruler. This means that there is electricity in the ruler. Ancient peoples were aware of this strange fact, but it is only over the last 200 years that we have really learned how to control electricity. Nowadays it powers thousands of appliances which are of enormous help to us all.

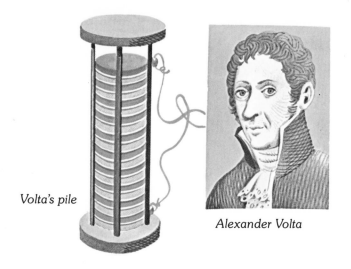

Volta's pile

Alexander Volta

Street Cars — Engines work by electricity as well. The first electric street cars were built during the last century.

Volta's Pile — The first person to produce and utilize electricity was Alexander Volta. He built a pile made of layers of disks composed of different kinds of metal, washed by an acid.

Light Bulbs — Then light bulbs were invented, which lit up when electricity reached them through a fine filament. Here are some old-fashioned bulbs.

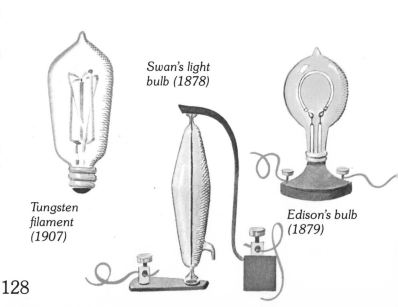

Swan's light bulb (1878)

Tungsten filament (1907)

Edison's bulb (1879)

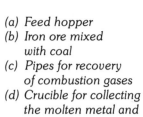

(a) Feed hopper
(b) Iron ore mixed with coal
(c) Pipes for recovery of combustion gases
(d) Crucible for collecting the molten metal and where the electrical discharges take place

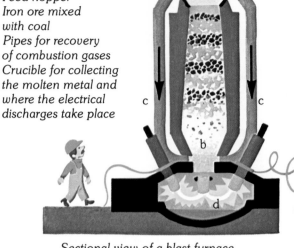

Sectional view of a blast furnace

Smelting — Under certain conditions, electricity can generate terrific heat. It is used in blast furnaces to smelt ores and also in steelmaking.

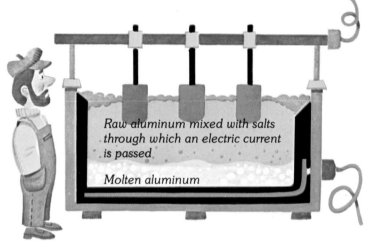

Raw aluminum mixed with salts through which an electric current is passed

Molten aluminum

Electrolysis — Pure metals can be obtained using electricity. The ores are placed in special tanks containing acids and salts and an electric current is passed through the tanks. Aluminum is obtained in this way.

Transport — Cable cars and ski lifts are worked by electricity too. A list of all the uses that this wonderful force has would fill several books.

Radio waves

Telecommunications — It's electricity that works the miracle which allows us to listen to a voice over the telephone or radio.

Building Sites — Many kinds of hard labor are made easier by electricity. Electric motors help huge cranes lift heavy loads and work the big cement mixers on building sites.

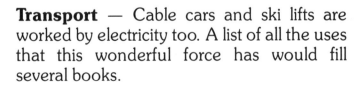

The Wonder Of Light

In The Night — At night thousands of lights twinkle all over the city. Street lights, illuminated signs, house windows and car headlights glow. Try to imagine for a moment what a city would be like without any light at night! What would happen if the sun didn't shine by day? There would be no life, for plants would not grow, the animals would have nothing to eat. How would man exist if there were no plants or animals? Light and heat are precious gifts provided by the sun and fire, yet man has been able to create artificial light and use it for many wonderful things.

Traffic Lights — A very important kind of artificial light signal is the traffic lights that control the traffic at busy junctions.

Signals — A very ancient way of sending messages was by waving flaming torches or lighting bonfires on hilltops. Roman soldiers used fire to send signals from one fort to the next.

The Lighthouse — Another very old way in which fire was used is the lighthouse, which sent out its signals at night to warn sailors of danger or showed the way into a port.

At The Airport — Artificial lighting is used to guide airplanes and ships at night. When a plane approaches an airport in the dark, the whole length of the runway is illuminated.

130

Photography — Two things which would not work without light are photography and the moving picture. In order to get a picture, light is allowed to enter the camera through the shutter and fall on the substances that cover the unexposed film.

Typesetting — Light is very important when it comes to typesetting books and newspapers. Lead letters are no longer required. A light beam imprints the words on to sensitive paper, rather like when taking a photograph, and the typeset articles are fed from the machine at high speed.

This is how the picture is exposed on the film

The Periscope — Some very important optical instruments make use of light. One of the most interesting is the periscope. The sailor can see what is happening on the surface when the submarine is under water through a series of reflecting mirrors.

The Secrets Of Matter — With the aid of light man has succeeded in discovering many of the secrets of matter. Every heated object gives out a different light. By studying the light from the stars and distant planets, scientists have found out what these heavenly bodies are made of.

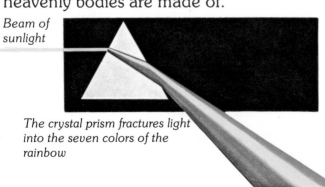

Beam of sunlight

The crystal prism fractures light into the seven colors of the rainbow

Inside the periscope

131

The Wonder Of Sound

The Orchestra — These children have always listened to music from the radio, records or tapes. They have never seen a live orchestra play before. It is wonderful to watch so many musicians together on the stage, each with his or her own instrument, and to listen to them play, led by the conductor. So many different sounds — yet what beautiful music comes out! One of man's magical achievements is that of turning sounds into music.

String Instruments — When a string is vibrated, it will emit sounds that may be high, low, soft or shrill. The instruments you see below are of this kind.

See how a blade vibrates

Double bass

Violin

Viola

Cello

Vibrations — Objects that have some elasticity produce sounds when they are vibrated. If we vibrate a steel blade fixed to a clamp, we can hear the sound it makes. We are able to speak because our vocal chords vibrate in our throats. The sounds are then carried through the air to our ears and so we hear them.

Drums — Primitive man stretched an animal's skin tightly over a hollow trunk and beat it with his hands or a stick. Nowadays, there are many kinds of percussion instruments, that is, musical instruments which make a noise when banged. Here are some on the right.

Triangle

Tympani

Cymbals

Drum

Bass drum

Ultrasounds — Certain substances can vibrate at such a speed that the sounds they produce are inaudible to man. Ultrasound is used in instruments that can distinguish obstacles in the fog.

Ultrasounds

Sonars — Other ultrasonic instruments on ships are used to measure the depth of the sea, or to locate large schools of fish. The exact distance between the target and the ship is calculated on the time taken for the ultrasounds to reach the target and return to base.

Wind Instruments — These instruments only make a noise when air is blown into them. The air vibrates little blades inside them.

Flute

Trombone

Trumpet

Saxophone

Tuba

Clarinet

Horn

Oboe

Bassoon

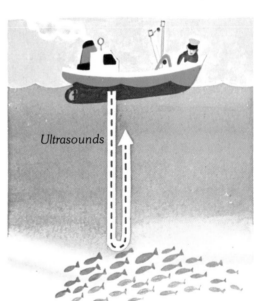

Ultrasounds

Noise Kills — Some sounds can be very pleasant, but can be dangerous when too loud and erratic. Our ears can only bear a certain level of noise. Noise can make people ill or deaf. Even music, if it is loud enough, can harm us.

133

Gravity

The Sling — Primitive man made use of centrifugal force without realizing it. He invented the sling to hurl stones at his enemies or dangerous animals.

Centrifugal force

Butter — A butter churn works on the centrifugal principle too. Butter is separated from the more liquid parts of milk in a churn. As the churn turns, the butter is whirled away from the center and accumulates on the walls.

Spin Dryer — Most washing machines have a special program for drying the clothes. A cylinder with tiny holes spins round and the water is thrown out through the holes.

They Don't Fall Off — Look at a globe and you'll see what the earth looks like. Now imagine that it is populated by many tiny people. Those at the north have their heads upward, but those down south look as though they are standing upside down. Why don't they fall right off the surface of the earth? There is a force called gravity which attracts all objects toward the center of the earth. Because of this, everyone's feet are kept firmly on the ground. This is the force that makes pebbles drop back to the ground after we throw them into the air. But there are other forces too that do strange things. For example, centrifugal force throws anything moving in a circle away from the center point. This force is responsible for some very odd things!

Washing machine with spin dryer

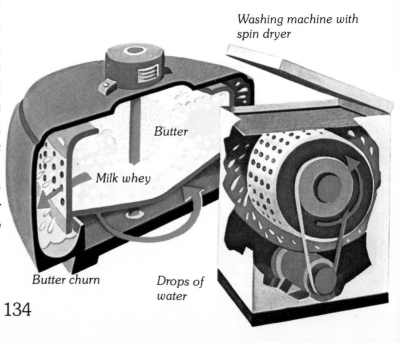

Butter

Milk whey

Butter churn

Drops of water

Car Tires — This force can be dangerous sometimes. If you take a bend too quickly, your car will tend to go straight on and run off the road. This is due to the effect of centrifugal force acting with other forces. The tires must have a good grip on the road so that the friction they generate will keep the car going the way you want it to. This is another example of man's cleverness in controlling the forces of nature.

Before Colanders — You may have seen someone drying lettuce by wrapping it in a tea towel and shaking it vigorously with a circling movement of the arm. Again, the centrifugal force throws out the water, leaving the lettuce dry.

Centrifugal force tends to make the car run off the road

The tire treads adhere to the road surface and help to avoid skidding

Rollercoaster

Man-made Satellites — Man uses the forces of nature when he keeps artificial satellites in orbit. What makes them spin round the earth without falling? They have reached a point of perfect balance between two different forces: gravity, which drags them toward the ground, and the centrifugal force which pushes them farther away from the earth round which they are traveling. Man has regulated their speed, height, weight and route so that the two forces are even and one does not become stronger than the other. In this way, the satellite continues on its path without crashing or flying off into space.

The Rollercoaster — Now we know why the cars on the rollercoaster do not drop off when they're upside down. The centrifugal force is so strong that they are kept firmly in position on the rails.

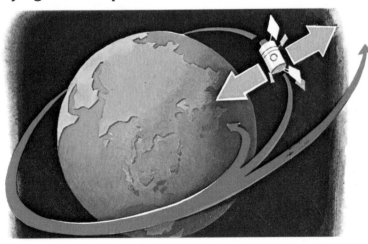

See how the action of twin forces keeps the satellite constantly in its orbit

Solar Energy

A Shortage Of Energy — Ever since man appeared on earth, but particularly in the last few decades, he has invented all kinds of machines. He will certainly invent others in the future. However, all new machines need energy before they will work. The great problem for the future will be to find new sources of energy for machinery which will benefit all of mankind. Everyone knows that oil, now the most convenient source of energy, will one day be exhausted. The same thing will happen to coal and methane. The only energy source that will not run out in the forseeable future will be the sun. This is why scientists have been trying hard to find a way of harnessing solar energy and turning it into electricity. They have partly succeeded. On the right you can see a huge solar furnace, one of the first set up in France, which can reach incredibly high temperatures just by directing the sun's rays on to a single spot. Many other ideas have become reality. Here are some.

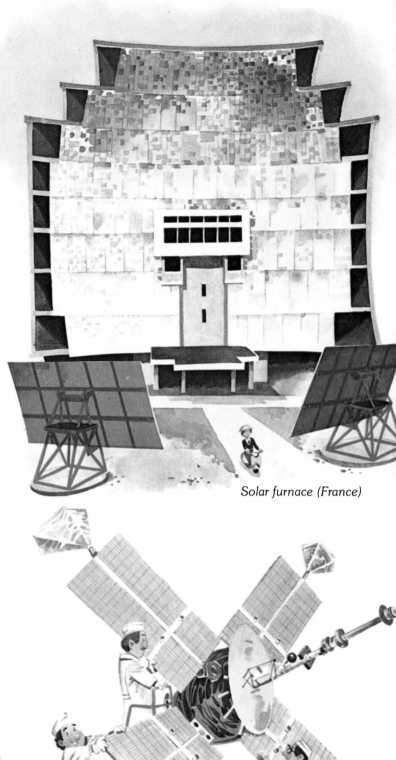

Solar furnace (France)

Reflectors — These gigantic mirrors follow the movement of the sun and concentrate the heat they collect toward a single water tank. In this way the water boils and generates steam. Under pressure, the steam works the turbines in a power station. The heat of the sun has become electricity.

Panels — Another way of turning the sun's heat into electricity is that used by spacecraft designers. Satellites are equipped with special panels which store heat to supply energy during the flight.

On The Rooftop — Entire villages have houses roofed with sun panels instead of ordinary tiles. In this way, they have a constant supply of hot water and electricity from the sun.

Camping Sites — People who take their vacations in caravans often make use of solar energy without realizing it. The hot water and electricity for many camp sites are obtained by the use of sun panels.

Mission To Mars — Space panels are continually undergoing improvement. One day they will capture enough energy from the sun to drive a huge spaceship 600 feet (200 meters) long, that will be able to land on Mars.

Mass-produced Panels — With the information gained from space launchings, panels and collectors are now being mass-produced, so that any factory can use them to generate energy from the sun.

Further Progress — It is wonderful what scientists have been able to achieve using sunlight and solar energy, but new steps will certainly be taken in this field in the future. Panels will become more efficient and improvements will be made. The picture shows a new kind of sun panel that may one day be fitted to cars so that we no longer have to depend on gas.

Atoms

Splitting Matter — If we break a brick with a hammer and smash it into tiny pieces, we reach a point where the fragments are so small they really could not become any tinier. Scientists used to think that all matter could be broken down into minute particles, but there was a limit. They called the smallest particle into which matter could be split an "atom". They thought it was impossible to break it down any further. Then it was discovered that even atoms could be split, and that an enormous amount of energy was freed when this happened. What is more, the particles of broken atoms bombarded neighboring atoms, splitting them too, and causing a chain reaction known as the "atomic reaction". After years of study, this discovery led to the building of the atomic bomb.

Nuclear Arms — The first atomic bombs could destroy whole cities in a matter of seconds. Since then, even more deadly weapons have been developed. Below you can see the "atomic mushroom", the column of smoke that rises after an atomic explosion. Many countries are trying to control the development of nuclear weapons.

Sectional view of a thermonuclear plant

Nuclear Submarines — These submarines' engines use atomic energy. On the left is a submarine that can sail around the world underwater without needing to refuel.

Welding

Measuring radioactivity present in plants that have been fed radioactive chemical fertilizers

In Industry — Atomic energy has many peaceful uses. In industry, for example, atomic radiation is utilized to check metal castings for faults and to ensure perfect welding.

In Agriculture — Certain by-products from splitting the atom are used in the study of plant behavior and for crop improvement. This scientist is watching how radioactive chemical fertilizer has affected the plants.

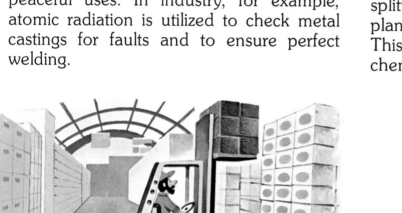

Food Conservation — Vegetables are prevented from germinating, fermenting and rotting when treated with a harmless amount of atomic radiation.

Finding The Age Of Objects — Ancient rocks and objects found on archaeological sites need to be given a date. This can be discovered with a special apparatus that measures even the faintest radiations emitted by the atoms inside these objects.

This scientist is handling radioactive materials with a set of mechanical hands, and is protected by a screen so that he will not come into contact with radiation

Danger — Material from nuclear plants must be handled very carefully, as it gives out radiations that can harm or kill living things. Scientists handle radioactive material with special apparatus to avoid being harmed by the radiation.

Atomic Energy

Atomic Power Stations — Many people believe in atomic energy and its capability to solve man's problems in the future. Yet many others are still against the construction of nuclear power stations that generate electricity through the use of atomic energy. "It's like piling atomic bombs in your own home," say those who disapprove. "Who can guarantee that one day a breakdown, a mistake or sabotage won't result in an explosion, causing a terrible disaster?" There is some risk, but the way our life has developed means that we need more and more energy and, apart from the sun, only the atom will be able to provide it when all the other sources have been exhausted. That is why nuclear power stations are now being built even though they pose some disturbing problems. On the other hand, these vast reactors are being made increasingly safer. Everything is now computerized. Above, you can see the control room of an atomic power station which generates electricity for a large city. Only two technicians are needed to control all the operations.

New Kinds Of Food — We shall get more than electricity from nuclear power stations. Atomic radiation can change the appearance of plants, so new fruit and vegetables can be obtained. Here are some plants being subjected to atomic radiation as an experiment. This system has already been used to develop new varieties of cereals that can withstand drought.

New Materials — Heat and atomic radiation can even change the properties of matter itself. With this machine, for example, scientists can turn coal into industrial diamonds.

Russian atomic-powered ice-breaker

New Ventures — Atomic energy can also help to change the face of the earth. For example, people are now talking of building another canal between the Pacific and Atlantic Oceans, parallel to the Panama Canal. It took 20 years to build the Panama Canal, but it would take only a few weeks with atomic energy. Above, you can see what the result would be like.

Engines — Cars, trains, ships and submarines will one day be equipped with atomic engines. Even today a small number of submarines and special ships are using atomic energy. But we shall have to wait for smaller and safer engines to be built before they are installed in transport such as cars.

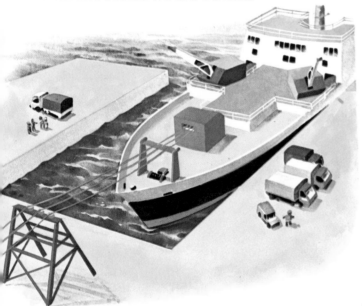

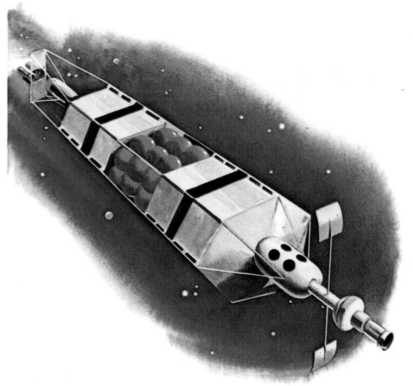

Rescue Work — In the future, atomic power units on ships could come to the rescue of cities hit by disaster, by immediately providing enough electricity to power the city's facilities.

Spaceships — Planes and spaceships will also be driven by atomic engines so that large quantities of spare fuel will not be needed. This is how a nuclear spaceship might look.

The Human Body

A Perfect Machine — Why do people become ill? The human body is a wonderful machine, but like all machinery it needs to be looked after correctly and fed properly. Even the most perfect of machines has to be repaired if something goes wrong with the works. The same thing happens to us. When our bodies break down for any reason we say we are ill. Once, doctors knew very little about the human body. Like a mechanic who is not familiar with all the parts of a machine, doctors were not quite sure how to go about repairing the bodily breakdown, that is, how to treat and heal it. Nowadays, however, every part of the human body has been studied closely and it has become much easier to cure a sick person.

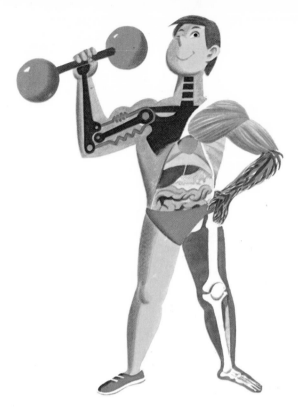

Muscles — The skeleton is covered with muscles which give the body its shape. Movement is made when they expand and contract. If the muscles have to work too hard, they may get injured which is painful.

Our Skeleton — The body is held together by the skeleton, which consists of more than 200 bones, each with its own function. If you break a bone when you are still young, it will heal perfectly as long as it is set properly.

The Nervous System — The nervous system controls muscular movement. Part of it receives orders from the brain while another part is independent and works without our being able to control it. The beating heart is an example.

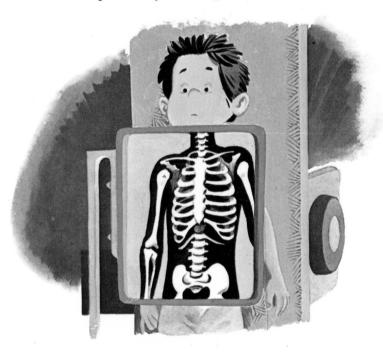

Any problems with your skeleton will show up on an X-ray

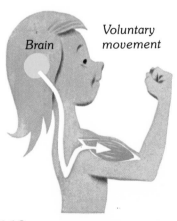

Brain — *Voluntary movement*

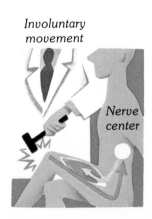

Involuntary movement — *Nerve center*

Blood — Every part of our body — bones, muscles and internal organs — is alive and needs food and oxygen. The blood carries both nutrients and oxygen throughout the body. Blood is pumped by the heart and circulates via the arteries and veins.

1 *Pituitary*

2 *Thyroid*

3 *Thymus*

4 *Surrenals*

5 *Pancreas*

6 *Sexual glands*

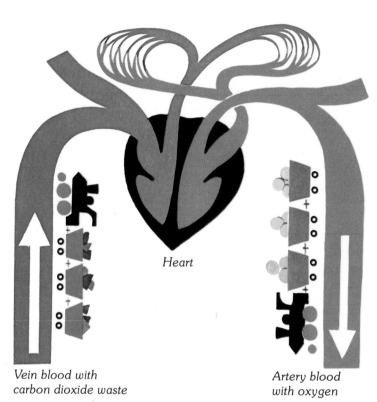

Heart

Vein blood with carbon dioxide waste

Artery blood with oxygen

The Glands — Our growth and behavior are regulated by a number of glands situated in various parts of the body. These work just like tiny computers. A knowledge of these organs is essential to prevent and cure many kinds of disease.

Respiration — Every time we breathe in the lungs filter oxygen from the air and pass it out to the blood. When it returns to the lungs again, the blood brings with it the waste from breathing. This is carbon dioxide and we breathe it out through the nose.

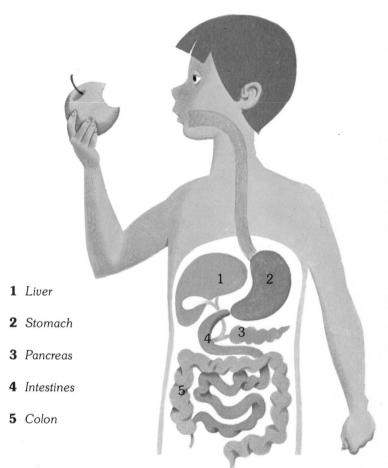

1 *Liver*

2 *Stomach*

3 *Pancreas*

4 *Intestines*

5 *Colon*

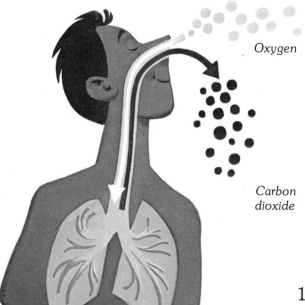

Oxygen

Carbon dioxide

Nutrition — Some of our internal organs digest (break down) the food we eat and pass all the nutrients and sources of energy we need into the blood. All these substances are distributed to the body by the arteries.

143

Time

5-4-3-2-1 Lift Off! — These experts are in the control room of Houston Space Center. They are controlling the launching of a missile. This is a time of intense concentration, for an error of just a fraction of a second could lead to the missile being launched on the wrong course or exploding in flight. The precise timing, down to the thousandth part of a second, is very important in this kind of work. Scientists have had to develop clocks that are absolutely exact in order to make interplanetary travel possible.

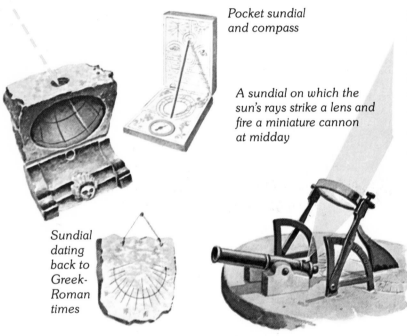

Pocket sundial and compass

A sundial on which the sun's rays strike a lens and fire a miniature cannon at midday

Sundial dating back to Greek-Roman times

Sundials — Primitive people learned how to measure the passage of time in days and months and they also invented the calendar. However, it was not easy to measure brief periods of time during the day or night. Sundials were the first method of measuring the hours. As the sun passed overhead a shadow moved over the sundial. The direction of the shadow showed the hour. Here are some of these old sundials.

The Hourglass — Of course, sundials stopped being useful as soon as the sun set. And so hourglasses were devised to measure the passage of time. The most common were filled with sand. These, however, measured only very short periods of time, such as a few minutes. When all the sand had flowed into the lower half of the glass, a definite period time had passed.

Hourglass   *Water clock*   *Oil clock*

Water And Oil — These two strange clocks are the work of ancient inventors. One is a water clock: a drop of water falls regularly into a pan, lifting a float linked to the hands of a clock. The other invention shows time, measuring the amount of oil burned by the lamp.

The Moors chime the hour at the top of this Venetian tower

A mechanical clock

A huge clock tower, Graz, Austria

An 18th century English clock; a lens projects the face on to the wall

The Mechanical Clock — Mechanical clocks were first made four centuries ago, and were very large. You can see on the left above one of the oldest.

Clock Towers — The earliest mechanical clocks were placed in clock towers or church steeples. Some of them had mechanisms which moved a group of figures whenever the hour was struck. One of the most famous is the Moors chime in Venice, Italy.

Table clock (Germany, 1575)

Enamelled watch (1630)

Swiss pocket watch (1580)

Look at this unusual clock: on the hour, the little bird sings and a tiny fountain begins to play

This Austrian clock (1665), slowly rolls down this slanting rod, but the hand does not slip. The mechanism works using the force of gravity

The Strangest — Clockmakers took much delight in making bizarre models, and some of the strangest are shown above.

Smaller And Smaller — As clockmaking techniques improved, clocks grew smaller and smaller in size, until table clocks finally gave way to watches.

In The Street — The first electric clocks were built 100 years ago, and all the clocks you see in the streets are worked by electricity. A single centralized engine feeds the movements to the hands. You can see these clocks on the far left.

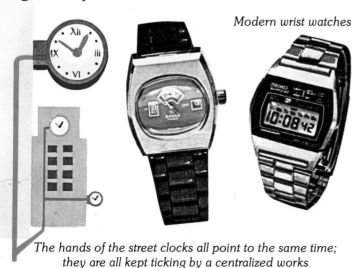

Modern wrist watches

Digital Watches And Clocks — Many wrist watches and clocks are now made without hands, and the minutes and seconds click on and off a small screen. There is no interruption in the measurement of the time. The most modern watches are electronic or quartz, and the most accurate are atomic.

The hands of the street clocks all point to the same time; they are all kept ticking by a centralized works

Writing

Pictographs — Long before writing was invented, primitive men used to carve or paint stories on rock. The first kind of writing consisted of figures and objects, and each of these had its own meaning. These rock carvings were made 10,000 years ago.

Ideographs — It was not always easy to express thoughts or convey a fact through drawings. Some countries, such as China and Egypt, developed simplified forms of signs to convey certain meanings. For example, a bent leg meant "run" and an eye meant "see". Here are some of these ideographs, which are also known as hieroglyphics.

Frescoes — In the Middle Ages, there were practically no schools, and only the sons of the rich were taught to read by private tutors. Huge paintings showing events in the life of Jesus were painted on the walls of churches. These frescoes covered the walls and were the only way that many people could learn at that time. Very few books existed and those that did were copied by hand. However, by means of the paintings those people who went into the churches could learn important things.

Egyptian hieroglyphics

(chair symbol)	*P*	Chair
(reeds symbol)	*S*	Reeds
(pleated fabric symbol)	*Y*	Pleated fabric
(hand symbol)	*D*	Hand
(mouth symbol)	*R*	Mouth
(owl symbol)	*M*	Owl

Chinese ideographs

Primitive form	Later form
(moon primitive)	(moon later)
	Moon
(earth primitive)	(earth later)
	Earth
(pray primitive)	(pray later)
	Pray
(tree primitive)	(tree later)
	Tree

146

The Phoenicians used cuneiform characters for writing

Cuneiform Characters — Ideographs were soon simplified even further, so that it was easier to write them. As time passed, the original figure gradually changed out of all recognition. Words, actions and ideas were expressed by wedge-shaped signs grouped together and arranged in a set form. These Sumerian tables of 6,000 years ago are a good example.

In China — The Chinese and Japanese languages are the only ones which still make use of ideographs.

A table of alphabets. From top: Phoenician, Greek capitals, Greek small letters, modern European, Ancient Latin and Cyrillac

The Rosetta Stone

The Alphabet — The Phoenicians completely altered the way of writing. Instead of using a sign for each name and action, they invented a symbol for every sound that goes to compose a word, just as we do today. The word "ant", for example, consists of the sounds "A N T" and we write a letter for each sound. Before, one sign was used to indicate the insect. The Phoenicians' invention quickly spread to other countries. This vital discovery of the alphabet meant that any word could be put down in writing. This was done with the use of no more than about 20 signs, or letters. All the existing alphabets have been derived from the Phoenician letters.

The Rosetta Stone — The stone illustrated above is one of the most important discoveries made in the history of archaeology. The text is carved in hieroglyphics and letters. By comparing the two kinds of writing, it finally became possible to read the meaning of hieroglyphics, which until then had been a complete mystery.

The Blind — Blind people can read by using a special raised writing known as Braille. This was invented by a Frenchman called Louis Braille.

The reader passes her fingers over raised dots arranged to represent the different letters of the alphabet and numbers

Mathematics

٠٩٨٧٦٥٤٣٢١

The Arabs — Each ancient civilization had its own system of calculation and writing numbers. However, traders who traveled from one region to another had difficulty in making themselves understood. Then the Arabic way of calculating and numbering spread to other countries and is now used throughout the world. The numbers we use today are known as Arabic numerals.

Pocket Calculators — Most people have one of these little calculators which can do even the most complicated sums and yet can fit into the palm of your hand. It is so easy to tap out the numbers on the keyboard that children can use it. Yet only a few years ago, pocket calculators not only didn't exist, nobody had thought of them. When a calculation had to be made, it was worked out on an electric adding machine or calculating machine. These are still found in one or two offices but they are large and clumsy and less efficient.

Abacus

Napier's machine

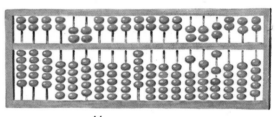

In Olden Days — Mathematics as a science has certainly come a long way since the time when people counted on their fingers. The first books that told of numbers and figures were clay tablets written by the Sumerians. Their contents included the rules to follow when measuring the surface area of fields, and some were used as trading ledgers.

Pascal's machine

Machines — The Chinese were using the abacus over 2,000 years ago, but real calculating machines were invented much later. Here are some of the oldest ones.

Weights And Measures — Each ancient people had its own system for weighing and for measuring length, and this made it difficult for merchants who had to deal with many different systems. Then certain countries began to use a fixed unit of measurement such as the meter, liter and kilogram. This is called the decimal system and practically all the nations of the world now use it.

This is the original kilo weight (Paris), protected by two glass bells so that it cannot be influenced by atmospheric conditions, such as changes in temperature, which could alter its characteristics

With Science — For more than 2,000 years, mathematicians had not done more than widen their knowledge of numbers and geometrical figures. Just a century ago, people began to realize that mathematics could be a great help in developing other branches of science.

Banks — Mathematics and its many uses make work so much easier in banking, industry and commerce.

Statistics — Mathematics has greatly expanded and is applied by those who prepare charts and statistics.

Computers — The mathematical operations needed nowadays to solve all the problems that crop up have become very complex. For this reason, the electric calculator has been invented. This is the computer, that can work out entire mathematical operations in a matter of seconds. It would take one person months of hard work to achieve the same result.

Newspapers

The Daily Paper — Many children would like to be journalists and work on a newspaper when they grow up. Some people think that writing for a paper is like being the sort of reporter you see in the films, always flying off from one continent to another, having exciting things happen to them, investigating and being the first to capture the criminals. It's different in real life. Special correspondents who report from disaster areas or war zones are only a part of the newspaper organization, and most newspaper reporters have a much less adventurous life. Many spend most of their time in the office, receiving news, rewriting their articles, writing headlines and preparing copy for the typesetters. A newspaper could not be printed at all without the skilled help of typesetters and other workers who set the manuscripts into pages of type and then high speed machinery transforms it into print.

Services — Every newspaper is divided into departments, each with its own head. The executive editor coordinates the various services and makes decisions when the managing editor is not available.

Entertainments editor

Sports desk

Economics expert

The Reporters — Each reporter is a specialist, either in the arts and entertainment, sport, crime or economics. The special correspondents roam the world following the best stories.

Managing editor

Journalist

The Managing Editor — Every newspaper has a managing editor, and he or she decides with the staff what news will make the headlines and how much importance is to be given to the rest.

Special correspondent

Local Correspondents — The major papers have local correspondents in all the big cities of the world, who send in articles reporting important events in that country.

The News — News items reach the editorial offices by phone, radio or telex. Staff editors then sort them out, often rewrite them and prepare titles. A special telephoto machine transmits photographs.

The Pages — Special staff make up the pages, fitting every picture and article into the space allotted. When there is too much text, it is shortened to fit into the space.

Page Layout — The corrected text is then arranged to form pages, in accordance with instructions from makeup staff. The executive editor passes the final layout and it is sent to the printer, where the newspaper is rolled off.

Typesetting — All the copy and titles, with a note of the style of type to be used and size of columns, is passed to the typesetting department. Lead characters were once used, but nowadays this operation is almost always done by phototypesetting.

Printing — Newspapers are printed on rotary presses which work at a high speed. As they come off the press, the papers are sent to the dispatch department which delivers them to news stands, street sellers and offices which employ newsboys who deliver the morning paper to each house.

Proof Readers — After the copy has been set, proofs are read and corrected in the proof readers' room. Spelling mistakes and wrongly-set lines are corrected and when necessary, special instructions given to the phototypesetting computer.

Recording

Fairy Tales — Long ago, grandmothers told children all those lovely fairy stories and they listened wide-eyed. Whenever Granny stopped for breath, the children would chorus, "More, more." But now grownups seem to have less and less time to tell stories. That is why you find records of fairy tales in the shops. The children sit in their room, switch on the record player and listen to a faraway voice saying, "Once upon a time . . ." They have beautifully illustrated story books to look at while they are listening, and the fairy tales have a musical background as well.

Portable record player

The Grooves — Records were invented long before cassettes and magnetic tapes. The sound signals which reach the record from the microphone are turned into wide or narrow grooves, which are deep or shallow, cut into the record itself.

The Mold — Records are produced in a special mold which reproduces all the grooves perfectly. A special kind of plastic is then laid between the two faces of the mold, which is heated and pressed until it takes on the exact shape of the mold.

Grooved surface of the record   *Needle head*

The Needle — When you listen to a record, you have to lower a special needle, known as a pick-up, into the grooves. This needle picks up each tiny section of the groove and reproduces the sound, which is then amplified by loudspeakers.

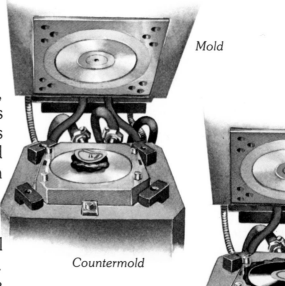

Mold

Countermold

Revolutions — There are big and small records, which play at different speeds. Some time ago, all records turned on the turntable at a speed of 78 revs per minute. Now, they almost all turn at a speed of 45 or 33 revs per minute.

152

High Fidelity — The best musical records are the high fidelity kind. As you listen to them, you feel you are right beside the orchestra. When the music is recorded, a number of microphones are placed at different points in the studio. Then all the sounds are united in two groups which are transferred on to the record using special techniques.

Discotheques — We can listen to any orchestra or band we like on our home record player. Because of this, many people have stopped going to concerts to listen to good music. If you want to dance now, you do so to recorded music. Discos are very popular with youngsters these days.

The Record Of The Future — This record has been produced using revolutionary techniques. The face of the record is molded to form a single unbroken spiral line composed of a series of dots and dashes. The surface is then covered with a film to protect it from dust and scratches, making it practically non-perishable. The recorded lines are read by a laser beam which brings out the sound of the music.

Loudspeaker box

Player deck

Amplifier

This is the surface of a record enlarged to 5,000 times its normal size

Record Players — Special pick-ups are required for stereo records, and amplifiers have to be placed in various positions so that the music comes from different parts of the room.

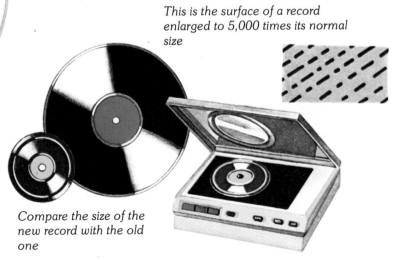

Compare the size of the new record with the old one

Photography

On The Walls — We are all used to seeing streets plastered with posters, bills and advertisements, huge figures looming out at us publicizing consumer products or the latest film. Probably no one notices that most of these are simply blown-up photographs. Had photography never been invented, then the walls in our cities would have an altogether different appearance.

Right: you can see how the image is reproduced upside down inside the camera obscura

Mirrors

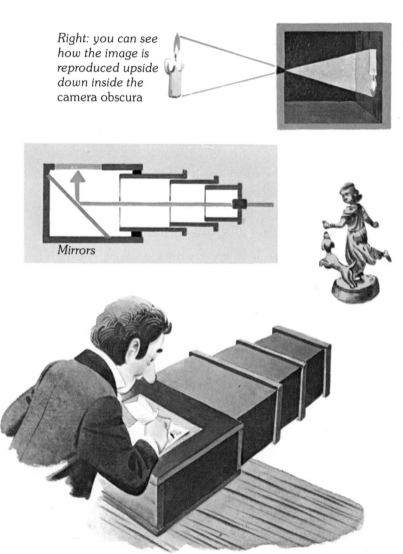

One of the first cameras, used by a Frenchman called Daguerre

Niepce's first photograph (1826) was of a village street

The Camera Obscura — The forerunner of the camera was a box like this, called a "camera obscura". Inside, there was a slanted mirror which reflected, in miniature, objects in front of the lens, on to a glass.

Glass And Silver — During the last century, a Frenchman named Niepce succeeded in printing the reflected image from a "camera obscura" on to a glass plate painted with salts of silver. This was the first photograph ever printed.

Small In Size — Niepce's invention was improved: materials with a higher sensitivity to light were discovered and used to cover the plate, and these early darkened box cameras became smaller. To the left is one of the first real cameras.

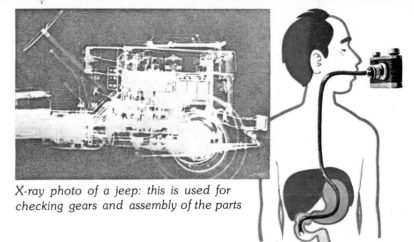

X-ray photo of a jeep: this is used for checking gears and assembly of the parts

The fibroscope (top right) is a flexible luminous fiber tube ending in a little bulb, and photographs can be taken inside a person's digestive system with this.

On The Paper — In the meantime, an Englishman called Talbot had found how to print photographs on to special sensitive paper. This is one of the first photographer's studios.

Cameras — Invention followed invention: cameras improved dramatically and more sensitive types of film were produced. Here is a range of modern cameras.

Color Photos — Fifty years ago the first negatives for color photography were produced. Even so, it was a long time before perfect colors could be obtained, and they were difficult to develop.

A cine film: the reel consists of a series of instant shots taken in rapid succession.

The Cine Camera — The cine camera was an offshoot of the camera, and a cine reel is a series of shots taken in rapid succession.

In Industry — Photography quickly turned out to be very useful in industrial processing and scientific research. Microscope photography, for example, enables us to study what materials are composed of and the characteristics of a product.

From The Sky — The colors on photographs taken from aircraft and satellites can tell us if a forest is diseased or a river is polluted.

Spies — Everything that is happening in any part of the world can be watched through high altitude photography. For this reason, the armed forces of every nation make ample use of aerial photography.

From The Moon — Photographs can now be sent across space from a great distance. Artificial satellites enable photographs taken on the surface of the moon to be received instantly on earth.

The Movies

The Inventors — Film-making was invented less than 100 years ago. The French brothers Lumiere were the first to produce a real movie in 1895. This is an old-fashioned camera.

Photographs — If photography had not been discovered, there would be no movies. Moving pictures are obtained by projecting transparent photograms made by taking 8 or 24 photographs per second, depending on the type of scene being filmed.

Memories — For a bit of fun, Dad has decided to show home movies which he took when he was young and had just met Mum. So the pictures of the times when they were engaged flash on the screen showing them looking much younger, of course, and wearing clothes which are out of fashion. Then come some pictures of the children as babies, their first toys, tantrums and fun. If we did not have movies, it would be difficult to remember so many things from the past. Movies are a very valuable means of communication because they are also a way of passing on our experiences to others, of recording events and studying what happens in Nature.

Part of the film on which the sound track has been recorded

The Sound Track — The first movies were silent. Then it was found that a series of signals like those of music cassettes could be applied to one side of the roll of film. Special machines then turned the signals into sounds. In this way, the voices, sounds and music accompany the pictures.

Three projection cabins

Branches brush the actors' faces as though they were really in a wood

Color — Color photography was invented later and this new technique was used for movies. Then came the wide screen Cinemascope. Nowadays techniques such as Cinerama and Technirama make movies even more spectacular.

Special Effects — Special effects and various tricks are often used. Here, you can see how a horseman pretends to ride through a forest scene set in a studio.

After Shooting — When Dad shoots a scene with his cine camera, all he needs to do afterward is to take the film to be developed. With professional movies, however, the work that follows shooting the film takes a long time. The words and music have to be added and the scenes joined together. It is slightly different when cartoons are being made; hundreds of drawings are needed for every minute of film shown. Each drawing is photographed separately and then the process is the same as for ordinary movies.

Film Making — Techniques for shooting a movie have changed enormously. The pictures show how scenes were shot when movies were first invented, and how they are shot today. Movie operators now have perfect equipment for the job. Some scenes are shot out of doors, but most movie making takes place at the studios where the scenery is built to create the proper backgrounds.

The Telephone

Under The Sea — When we speak into the phone, our voices are turned into electrical impulses which pass along the wires into the phone of the listener, where they are turned back into sounds. Once, words could only be transmitted through special cables. This meant that to enable telephone calls to be made to places overseas, great lengths of cable had to be laid on the sea bed to link the distant coasts. This was a difficult and skilled job which was done from special cable-laying vessels like the one in the picture. It was stacked with giant rolls of cable which were specially covered so that they did not become corroded. Transatlantic cables are no longer used. Telephone links are now made by radio waves and connections formed by man-made satellites. In less than 100 years, the telephone system has made giant steps which our grandparents would not think possible.

The rollers and wheels that are used to unwind cables are stored in the hold

Through The Air — Words travel from one city to another through the air. They pass along the telephone lines to antennas and are transmitted by radio waves to the terminal antennas. From these they go down the lines again to the receiver of the person we are speaking to.

Radio bridge connecting urban centers

Antenna for intercontinental communications

Urban center

Center

Along The Wire — In the city, the words we speak on the telephone travel along a wire, often laid underground. Hundreds of voices pass along special cables, without ever getting mixed up.

The Exchange — Telephone wires form an intricate net of lines. The telephone exchange channels each voice in the right direction.

Telephone exchange

Radio taxi

Bus driver

Telephone on the train

Connections — Telephone connections were once made by the exchange operators who put the two people in contact. This would be impossible nowadays, with the thousands of phone calls that are made each second. We now have the system known as direct dialing which gives us automatic contact with the number we dial.

The Radio Phone — This is very useful, especially for taxis, public transport and trains. You can also get a phone with television screen and see the person you are talking to.

The Telephones Themselves — The styles of phones have changed enormously in the last 100 years. Now, instead of dialing a number or pressing a button panel, you can insert a special card corresponding to the person's number. The phone does the rest.

Portable Phones — At the moment the very latest in phones is the pocket phone which fits into a handbag. This one was made in Japan.

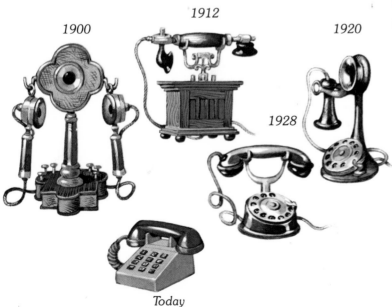

1900

1912

1920

1928

Today

Portable telephone

Radio And Television

The Television Studios — We get all kinds of programs on TV, from the news to documentary films, television plays and TV films. When we switch on to our favorite programs we hardly ever think of all the effort that has gone into producing them, and how many people have worked together to make them a success. This is also true of radio; although sound effects are important, the scenery does not matter because there is no picture.

The Reporters — Radio and television studios have editorial offices in the same way as newspapers do, where staff reporters work or send in their reports from other countries.

The Announcers — Every program is introduced by an announcer, who always has a pleasant smile. Announcers must have an attractive voice and speak very clearly.

Ballerinas

Actor

Presenter

The Actors — Actors, like those in films or on the stage, take part in plays. Other entertainers include ballerinas, singers, jugglers, and comedians. Even more important than the entertainers are the people who work behind the scenes, and don't appear on the screen. These are the organizers of the show, headed by the producer.

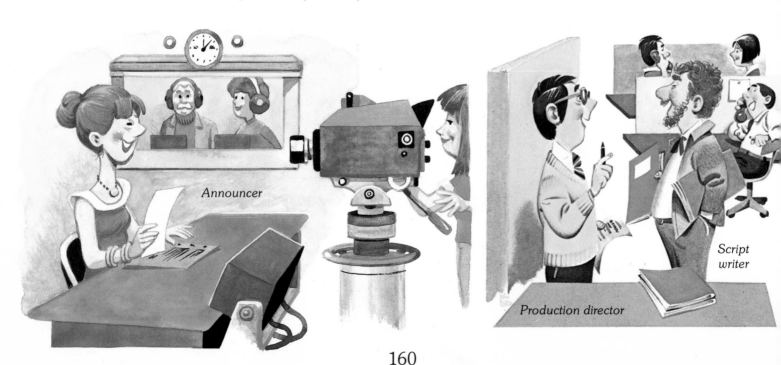

Announcer

Production director

Script writer

Choreographer

Lighting technician

Cameraman

Production secretary

Costumes expert

Producer

The Technicians — All sorts of people are needed, from the stage assistants to the interior decorators, the electricians and the special effects men. Then, when the cameraman starts to film, the light and sound operators and monitor assistants all set to work.

The Director's Cabin — While the transmission is taking place, the director sits in the monitor cabin with the technicians and an array of monitor screens. The scenes are filmed from different angles. Each picture flashes on to a monitor and the producer decides which is to be broadcast.

Production Staff — The producer must have a large number of staff if the show is to be a success. These include the script writer, the stage manager who is in charge of everything required for each scene, the production secretary who maintains staff contacts, the choreographer who arranges the dance scenes and costumes, and many more technicians.

Movies — It is much easier to broadcast a movie and fewer technicians are needed. All the work has been done when the movie was being shot and the sound track made, as for the movies.

The Sports People Play

The Champions — Can sport be regarded as work? It is for those who spend all day training for competitions and championships. Physical exercise is good for us all, which is why we have gym classes at school, but it is one thing to play sports just to keep fit, and another to try to become the very best at any particular sport. Sports champions follow hard training timetables laid down by team doctors and coaches, and their physical fitness is always under control.

Baseball — This sport is very popular in the United States. Two teams of nine men each play the game. Each team takes turns trying to hit a hard ball thrown by a pitcher from the opposing team. The object is to hit the ball where the opposing team can't catch it, in order to score a run. The team that scores the most runs wins the game.

Soccer — Only the goalkeepers can touch the ball with their hands during a soccer match. All the other players have to use their feet to kick the ball and try to get the ball into the goal.

Car Racing — Formula 1 races, with their very fast cars and special circuits, are a spectacular sight. Car racing is a dangerous, but exciting sport.

Tennis — The game of tennis has been played for many years. The match takes place on a rectangular court with a net stretched across the middle. Racquets are used to hit the ball, and each time a player does not succeed in returning the ball to the other side his or her opponent makes a point.

Gymnastics — This is one of the most popular sports particularly in the Olympic Games. To get to a high standard the gymnast has to train very hard with a training coach. Most of these coaches have been gymnasts themselves and when they retire from competition they become professional coaches.

Golf — The golfer tries to hit the ball with a special club into a small hole, taking as few shots as possible. A golf course generally consists of 18 of these holes.

Ice Skating — Skating is like dancing: it calls for graceful movements and a lot of practice. At first it is not easy to balance on the thin blades without falling.

Women's Bowling — Over the last 20 years ten pin bowling has grown in popularity. In America there are major professional leagues for both men and women.

Horse Racing — Some racehorses are worth thousands of dollars, but a good jockey is also needed to win a race. The jockey must know the horse he is riding and be able to win its confidence.

From Huts To Skyscrapers

Our House — These children live in a comfortable modern house and they could not even begin to imagine what life must have been like for the human race when nobody had learned how to build a wall. These children have central heating in winter, air conditioning in summer, large windows, which protect them from wind, noise, the damp and nasty insects and yet give them a view so clear that it is like living in the open. They have armchairs and comfortable beds and a bathroom with hot and cold water. They can switch on light and music. These things are all made possible as a result of progress. Once upon a time they did not exist.

1. *South-west Asia*
2. *Central Europe (Bronze Age)*
3. *African savannah*
4. *Central-South African jungle*
5. *Lapland (hut made of earth, wood and skins)*
6. *Scandinavia (log cabin)*
7. *North American Indian wigwam, covered with bark*

Early Shelters — Primitive men had no idea how to construct a building. They sheltered from bad weather inside a cave and slept under the trees, out of the wind. Then man learned to use branches and tree trunks to build a more comfortable and safer shelter. This was the first hut. There are still people in parts of the world who live in huts. The shape varies, for they are built according to the climate and with whatever materials are available.

164

Walls — Thousands of years ago men surrounded their villages with stone walls for protection. Later, the homes of important villagers were built with stone and mud and bricks.

Knossos palace, the island of Crete

An insula, storied building of ancient Rome

Medieval building of wood and brick

Buildings For All — The use of stone and bricks as building materials began to spread, especially in the cities. As time went on, most people had a proper home, solid and comfortable. Two thousand years ago, multistory brick houses like this were built in ancient Rome.

Higher And Higher — Then there became a shortage of space in the mediaeval walled cities. This led to the buildings being built upward, the only way in which more accommodation could be obtained.

Skyscrapers — Iron, reinforced concrete and steel made it possible for high-rise buildings to be erected. These have many floors. There is not much space available in cities for building, but a great deal of accommodation has to be found for homes and offices.

Prefabricated Buildings — Building techniques have changed a great deal. Instead of laying bricks on top of each other, the walls can be built in one section. These prefabricated sections are then assembled with the aid of cranes in a very short time.

165

Machines And Engines

A Game — Children love to take mechanical toys to pieces to see what they're like inside and find out what makes them work. All mechanical toys have a spring mechanism inside or a battery-run motor. Without this, they would not be able to move at all. Things stay where they are put unless they are on a slope and can slide down.

The Simplest Machines — These children are using a large stone as a rest, and a plank of wood as a lever to lift a box. By using the plank, they have given themselves more strength, and this is what machinery does. Even the lever is a sort of machine, the simplest in existence.

Engines Today — Man has succeeded in using many of the forces of nature in order to run machines. Here are some examples of the ways these forces are used.

Using a plank as a lever the children can easily lift the weight

The Winch — Other very simple kinds of machinery are pulleys and winches. We can use these to lift very heavy weights, since it is the rope that takes the strain.

Wind — Windmills with large arms or blades were built to harness the wind. In some country areas, you'll see sets of blades at the top of pylons. These turn in the wind and produce electricity for the local farms.

Water makes this wheel go round

This 'gearwheel' passes the movement on to the hammer

The Electric Motor — You can see how many different kinds of electric motors there are. They all work by the combined force of electricity and magnetism.

Water — Many years ago, men learned how to use the miller's wheel. This huge mallet is used for ironworking, and water is the force that makes it move.

Steam under pressure

Piston

Steam — This is a section view of a locomotive. The engine is worked by steam kept at high pressure in the furnace boiler.

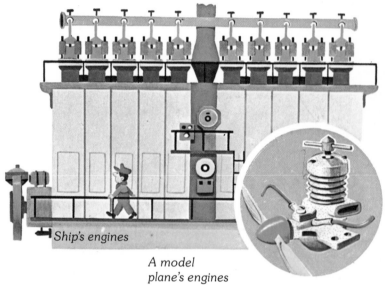

Ship's engines

A model plane's engines

Engines — Many different kinds of combustion engines have been built. They all utilize the sparking force from the mixture of fuel and air in their cylinders. Here is a large engine and a very small one.

The Atomic Engine — The latest type of engine is very powerful as it uses atomic energy. Atomic engines drive huge ships and submarines.

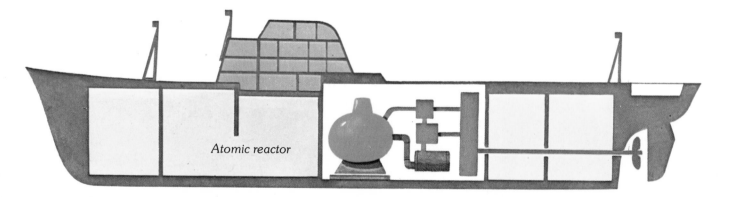

Atomic reactor

Cars Through The Ages

At The Wheel — Traveling is easy nowadays because many people own cars. Cars come in all makes and sizes: small, cheap, compact cars; family models; cars for people who travel a lot and for those who need to get to work, as well as luxury models with high-powered engines, telephones and refrigerators. When we see the number of cars around, it hardly seems possible that, not so very long ago, cars were rare objects. Cars are a recent development and have only been in existence for 100 years.

1905 French coupe

1910 saloon car

The Ford model T, mass produced between 1908-1927

The Engine — Before the first car could be built powerful engines that were lightweight as well as small had to be invented. Steam engines were no good. The combustion engine, which used explosive gases such as petrol vapor, was just right for this purpose. The first cars had a maximum speed of 8 miles (15 kilometers) per hour and were very noisy. Some countries insisted that a man waving a red flag had to walk in front of this strange vehicle.

The Bodywork — The engine was mounted on an iron frame and connected to the wheels. The wooden bodywork was built round this basic shape. Later, the bodywork was made of sheet iron. Then mass production of different models began and the large car manufacturers came into existence. As manufacturing techniques improved, the cost of cars began to fall.

Benz tricycle, 1888

Panhard, 1892

Duryea racing model, 1895

Lanchester, 1895

Renault, 1898

Rolls Royce, 1905

Studebacker, 1915

Mercedes sports car, 1928

Chrysler Airflow, 1934

The famous Volkswagen 'Beetle'

Fiat Brooklands, 1913

Union C car, 1936

Cars For All — Cars have changed in appearance over the years. However, it is only since World War II that the car has become really common. The first cars were only just on the road when speed and endurance racing began to take place. People can't help smiling nowadays when they look at pictures of the first racing cars. The cars that roar round the tracks today look very different from those of the early 1900s.

Ferrari T4

169

The Development Of Airplanes

Canvas And Wood — The first airplanes were a strange shape. They were made of canvas and wood, to keep them light and had only a few iron parts.

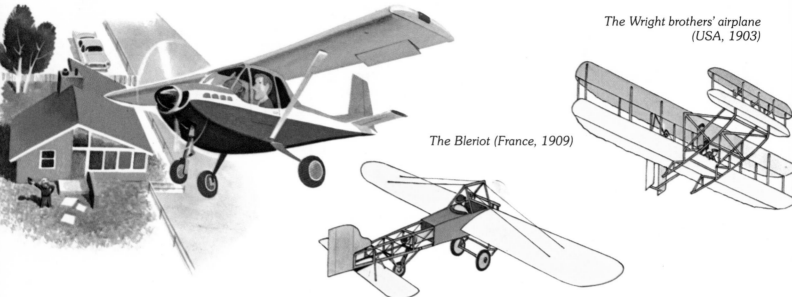

The Wright brothers' airplane (USA, 1903)

The Bleriot (France, 1909)

The Fokker E. (Germany, 1915)

The Caproni CA 33 bomber (Italy, 1915)

Like Cars — In some countries people use planes instead of cars to get from one place to another, especially where there are no roads and the land is either forest or desert. Short runways are laid close to the nearest town and the aero-taxis land and take off with the greatest of ease. They can operate under all conditions and it is nearly as easy to pilot a small plane as drive a car. Most people prefer to fly across the ocean now rather than go by ship. Yet 70 years ago no one could have imagined the progress that would take place in aviation.

In Battle — The early aircraft was not very stable, but brave pilots fought fierce aerial battles during World War I. Fighter planes and bombers were developed and improved.

Over The Ocean — Aircraft became faster and more powerful, and even succeeded in flying across the Atlantic. Lindbergh (left) was the first to achieve this.

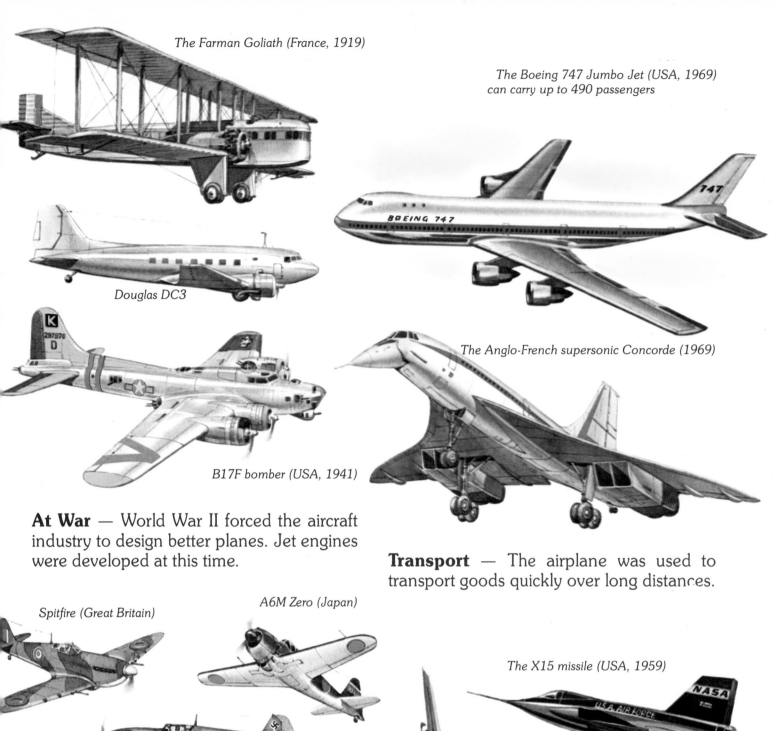

The Farman Goliath (France, 1919)

The Boeing 747 Jumbo Jet (USA, 1969) can carry up to 490 passengers

Douglas DC3

B17F bomber (USA, 1941)

The Anglo-French supersonic Concorde (1969)

At War — World War II forced the aircraft industry to design better planes. Jet engines were developed at this time.

Transport — The airplane was used to transport goods quickly over long distances.

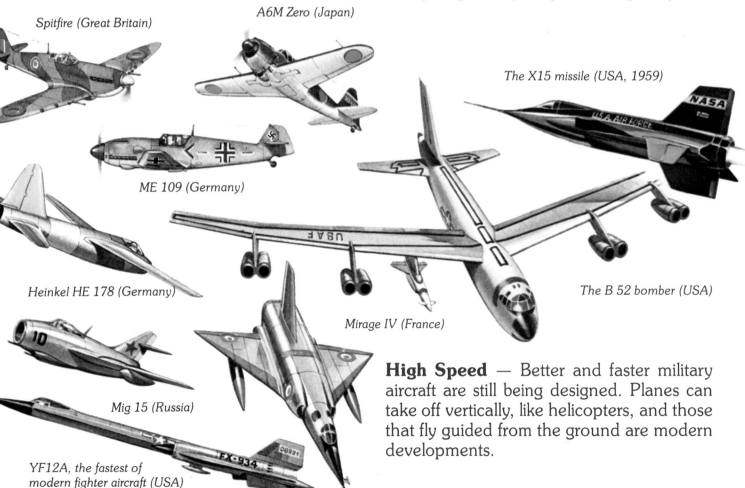

Spitfire (Great Britain)

A6M Zero (Japan)

The X15 missile (USA, 1959)

ME 109 (Germany)

Heinkel HE 178 (Germany)

The B 52 bomber (USA)

Mirage IV (France)

Mig 15 (Russia)

YF12A, the fastest of modern fighter aircraft (USA)

High Speed — Better and faster military aircraft are still being designed. Planes can take off vertically, like helicopters, and those that fly guided from the ground are modern developments.

How Ships Have Changed

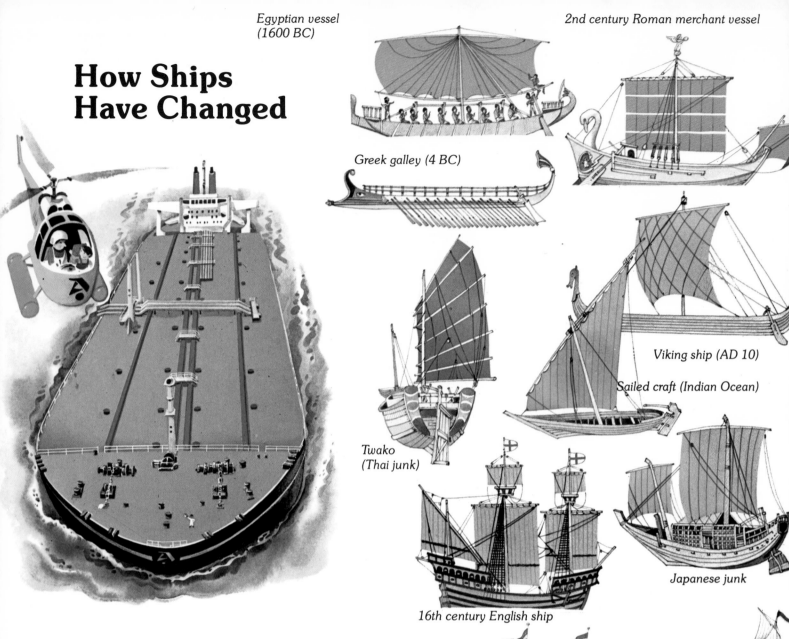

Egyptian vessel (1600 BC)

Greek galley (4 BC)

2nd century Roman merchant vessel

Twako (Thai junk)

Viking ship (AD 10)

Sailed craft (Indian Ocean)

16th century English ship

Japanese junk

The Oil Tanker — This is one of the biggest ships in the world. It is a giant that carries millions of tons of oil from the oil-producing countries to the consumer nations. Once, it took many tankers and hundreds of men to transport the same amount of oil. Ships have undergone great changes in recent times. The famous old passenger liners are disappearing because most people nowadays prefer to fly, but highly specialized ships are being built for specific forms of transport.

North European vessel (17th century)

18th century brig

In The Ancient World — The first boats were flimsy wooden craft that could not survive a stormy sea. They either had oars, sails to catch the wind, or both.

The Sailing Ships — As time went on, bigger ships were built which were still made of wood. They could often reach a good speed with several sets of sails.

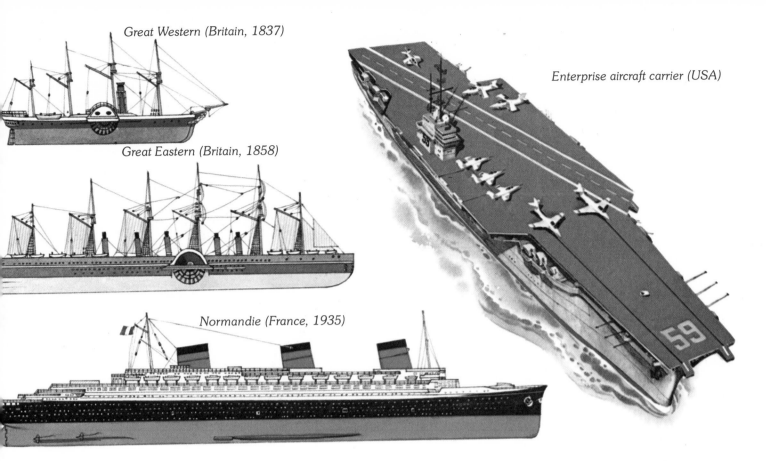

Great Western (Britain, 1837)

Great Eastern (Britain, 1858)

Normandie (France, 1935)

Enterprise aircraft carrier (USA)

Engines — Ships changed completely with the coming of steam, just as locomotives did. The first iron vessels were built. Ships' engines were quickly improved: the diesel was invented, then the electric and finally the atomic-powered engine.

Aircraft Carriers — A special kind of military vessel is the aircraft carrier. The deck has a runway so that planes can take off and land.

Special Ships — Modern vessels include those used for special purposes, such as the ferry, icebreaker and refrigerator ships.

Missile launching cruiser

Hovercraft

Naval Forces — Powerful craft have been built for use in wars. Armor-plated and equipped with many weapons, their size depends on the use to which they will be put.

Hovercraft — This vessel rises above the surface of the water because it rides on a cushion of air caused by powerful jets.

173

Underwater Travel

Experiments — Experiments have already been carried out on how to live under water. Scientists have tried living for weeks and even months in underwater houses such as these. In this way they can find out what the human body can put up with, and what it needs to adapt to surroundings that are totally different from those in the open air. These experiments are very important, so that in the future man can live and work at the bottom of the sea in order to search for oil and rare metals, or cultivate seaweeds and farm fish in coastal waters. Already, technological progress has enabled us to build experimental vehicles that travel underwater with passengers and freights. These vehicles will be improved in the future. There could even be underwater buses!

Submarines — Submarines became larger and more efficient, and the latest is driven by atomic power. Some of these can travel for months at a time.

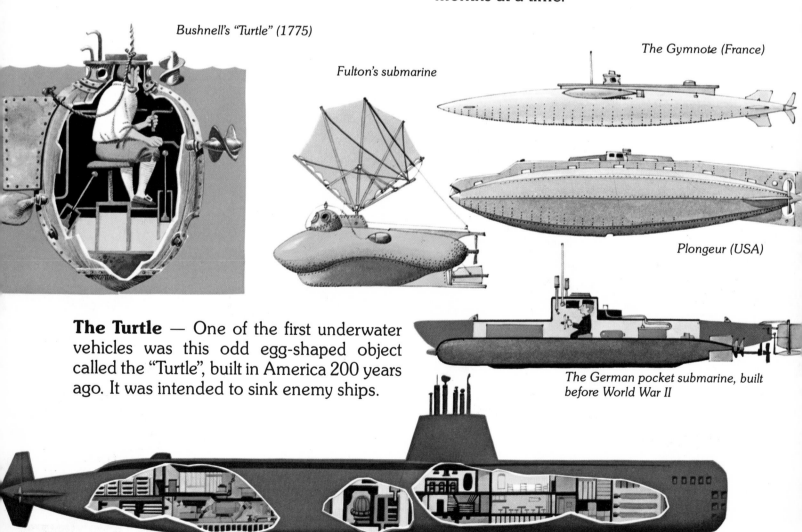

Bushnell's "Turtle" (1775)

Fulton's submarine

The Gymnote (France)

Plongeur (USA)

The Turtle — One of the first underwater vehicles was this odd egg-shaped object called the "Turtle", built in America 200 years ago. It was intended to sink enemy ships.

The German pocket submarine, built before World War II

The US nuclear submarine Nautilus

The Deep Diver — In 1967, a vehicle was built from which a person can emerge and reenter while underwater. It has a crew of four: two drivers and two divers. One day it will be very useful for salvage work.

The Ben Franklin — This is the name of the exploration submarine used for the first time by Jacques Piccard in 1969. It has traveled the length of the Atlantic Ocean at all depths.

Merchant Submarines — Some shipyards are designing special submarines to transport freight underwater. These will be able to pass under the polar ice-cap and shorten many trans-oceanic routes.

On The Sea Bed — Apart from these underwater transporters, there will be special tracked vehicles which can move across sand and mud on the sea floor. They will look like army tanks and have powerful headlights.

For Work — Other sea bed vehicles, linked to surface ships, will be used to remove and send minerals to the surface, such as manganese and nickel, which lie as pebbles on the sea bed.

Trains And Cars — One day we will be able to drive or travel by rail under the sea. Underwater tunnels, such as that linking France and Britain across the Channel, are now being studied.

Inside the Deep Diver

The Ben Franklin

The Channel Tunnel might look like this

Machine used to collect minerals from the sea bed

Food From The Sea

Underwater Farming — If the world population continues to grow as quickly as it is doing now, there will not be enough food to feed the people even if the whole face of the earth is covered with crops. We will have to look to the oceans to provide food, and not just fish, as we do at the moment. We will be obliged to farm fish, in the same way we breed hens and pigs. Special kinds of seaweed will have to be grown as fish food, and the ocean beds will become one vast expanse of aquafarms, like the one in the picture.

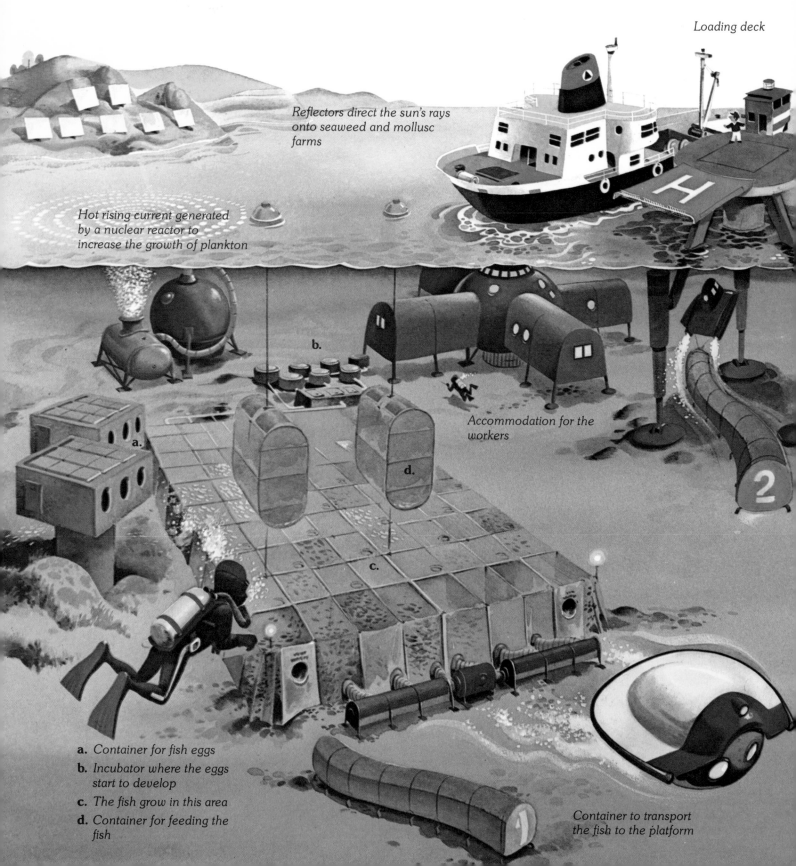

Loading deck

Reflectors direct the sun's rays onto seaweed and mollusc farms

Hot rising current generated by a nuclear reactor to increase the growth of plankton

Accommodation for the workers

a. *Container for fish eggs*
b. *Incubator where the eggs start to develop*
c. *The fish grow in this area*
d. *Container for feeding the fish*

Container to transport the fish to the platform

Seaweed — Certain kinds of weed, which are rich in nutrient and medicinal components, are already grown on underwater nets.

Molluscs — Mussels and other shellfish are being farmed today, but their numbers will increase in the future.

Fish Farming — Fast-growing fish are now being farmed in artificial freshwater ponds. One day the same techniques will be used in the sea.

Fishing — Newer and faster fishing techniques will be developed. This boat is pumping the fish aboard, after attracting them with lights and electric fields.

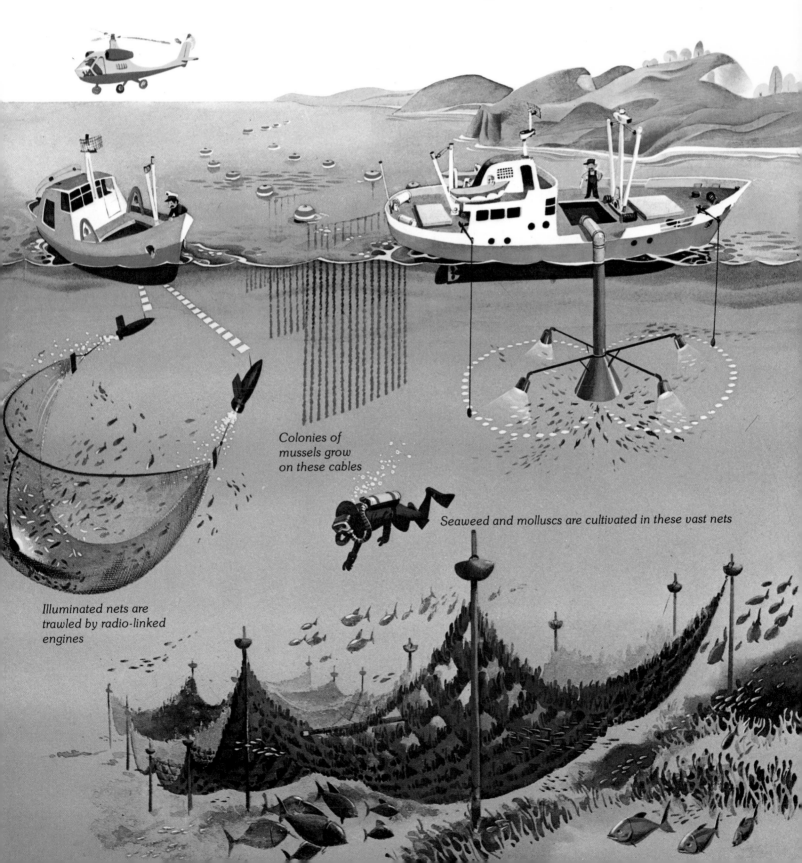

Colonies of mussels grow on these cables

Seaweed and molluscs are cultivated in these vast nets

Illuminated nets are trawled by radio-linked engines

Our World And The Universe

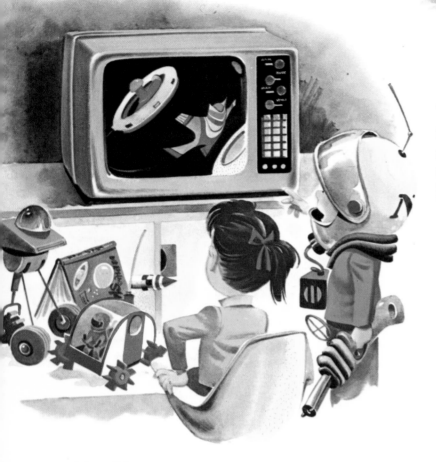

Travels — At some time in the past, adventurers must have gone on journeys of exploration and so it was discovered that the earth was huge. However, no one had found what lay across the apparently endless oceans.

The Universe — We now know that the earth is only a dot in the universe. Great numbers of other planets exist along with our own, and astronomers are continually finding others far out in distant space. Science fiction films no longer surprise us, because we know that they could become reality one day. We are quite used to watching programs on TV telling us of the wonders of the universe and showing photographs taken from spacecraft as they travel among the planets. We are lucky to have all this knowledge at our fingertips. Long ago people had come to all the wrong conclusions about space.

Primitive Man — Early man had no knowledge of any place beyond his own stretch of plains or mountains. He probably never even wondered where the water in the rivers came from, or what lay on the other side of the mountains. Ancient geographers thought the earth was flat, with dry land in the middle surrounded by the oceans. The picture shows what they thought the continents were like.

Reconstruction of a Greek map drawn by Heratosthene in 2 BC

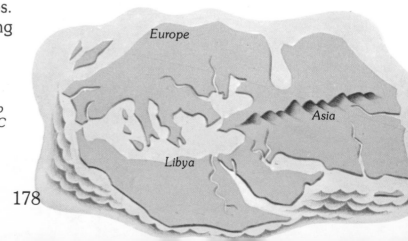

Europe

Asia

Libya

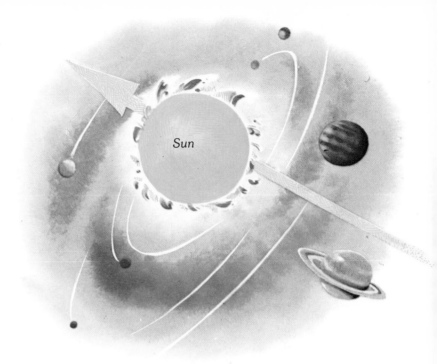

A Round Earth — It was proved that the earth was round when navigators sailed right around the world while exploring the then unknown continents.

Moving In Space — Today, we know that the earth and the other planets all travel around the sun. We also know that the sun itself is moving at great speed in the universe.

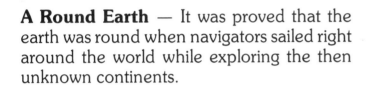

Men From Mars — Can there be life on other worlds that travel around other stars? There could be, but we do not know whether there is or not. We do know, however, that none of the other planets in our solar system has life on it. And the men from Mars, which so many people like to draw, do not exist.

Which Is Moving? — Now that they knew the earth was round, some people still asked questions. Does the sun travel around the earth each day, or is it the earth that travels around the sun?

Astronomy

An improved astrolabe

On The Roof — If you want to discover the wonders of the heavens it is not enough to watch the stars with the naked eye. So amateur astronomers buy small telescopes to look at the night sky, and set up a miniature observatory on the roof or balcony. Technology has now provided a large number of instruments for watching and photographing the stars. But long ago, astronomers had to make their own equipment in order to carry out their studies.

Eyesight — Other pieces of equipment improved on the astrolabe, but keen eyesight was necessary just the same. People still had to use their eyes to explore the skies.

The Astronomer's Glass — Great progress was made about 400 years ago when Galileo made the first astronomer's glass. When he looked through this, the stars seemed bigger.

An astrolabe of 1468

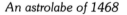

The telescope at Yerkes observatory, USA

The Astrolabe — This was one of the earliest instruments invented in ancient times for studying the stars. The ancients used it to calculate the height of the stars over the horizon and the distances between the stars.

The Telescope — Galileo's glass was the forerunner of modern telescopes. These enormous pieces of equipment are installed in observatories. They enlarge the stars, making them look thousands of times bigger.

The Giant — The biggest telescope in the world is on Mount Palomar, in the United States. Its glass mirror is 15 feet (5 meters) in diameter and weighs 15,680 pounds (750 kilograms).

Observatory at Mount Palomar

Satellites — Man-made satellites are also being used to study the skies. As the satellites orbit the earth, they pick up signals and take photographs from outside the barrier of the atmosphere that encircles the earth.

Photography — Certain telescopes are specially equipped for night photography. In this way, a chart of the heavens can be made, consisting of 2,000 pages and reproducing 25 million stars.

Binoculars — If you have nothing better, a pair of binoculars will do. Even with them the stars look bigger.

Radiotelescope

The Radio Telescope — The newest of all astronomical aids, the radio telescope, is like a giant ear that picks up electromagnetic signals from millions of miles away. So new stars giving out radio signals can be discovered, even though they cannot be seen.

The Moon

The Crescent Moon — It is pleasant to look at the moon on a clear, quiet evening. Sometimes the moon is not "full", and it looks eaten away; sometimes it is just a thin crescent. From earliest times man wondered about how and why the moon became thinner and thinner until it vanished, then started to grow again until it became a full, round ball. After observing the phases of the moon, primitive man made the first calendar and divided the year into months. In fact, a month is the length of time between one full moon and the next.

Close Up — Many things were known about the moon long before man arrived there with his spacecraft. For example, we knew that the moon is 236,120 miles (380,000 kilometers) from the earth, while the sun is 500 times farther away.

Darkness — The moon has no light of its own. It is a satellite of the earth, is made of rock and would be pitch-black were it not for the light of the sun that it reflects back toward us. In fact, when the earth passes in front of the sun and shades the moon, the moon disappears or is only partly visible.

The volume of the moon is fifty times less than that of the earth

If we take the distance from the earth to the moon as 1 inch (2 cm), the distance from the earth to the sun will be 60 feet (20 meters)

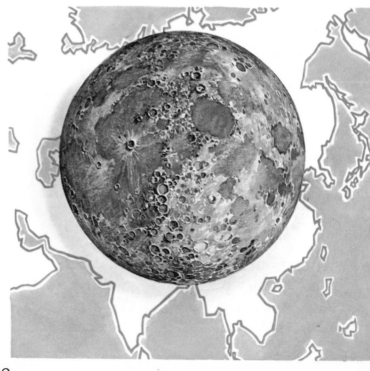

So Small — The picture on the right shows how small the moon is compared with the earth. Its diameter does not even cover a continent the size of Asia.

Earth

Around In A Circle — The moon moves around the earth, and the same side of the moon is always facing us. It takes 29 days to make a complete orbit. Until only a few years ago, when space exploration began, no one knew what the other side of our natural satellite looked like.

No Life — Space exploration has confirmed that there are no forms of life, either animal or plant, on the moon. There is neither air nor water; both of which are necessary for life.

The Rock — What the ancient astronomers once called the "lunar seas" are really vast, dusty plains, fringed by mountains that are sometimes 33,000 feet (10,000 meters) high.

This picture, taken from a photograph, illustrates the craters on the moon's surface

The Craters — The strangest thing about the surface of the moon is its craters. There are about 30,000 of these. The biggest are about 186 miles (300 kilometers) wide and up to 2,818 feet (7,000 meters) deep; some are quite small. We still do not know what caused them. They may be of volcanic origin, or they may have been formed when great blocks of rock (meteorites) from distant universes crashed into the moon. Another possibility is that the craters were bubbles formed on the lunar crust, which later exploded as the crust cooled. Perhaps all these things helped to give the moon's surface its pitted appearance.

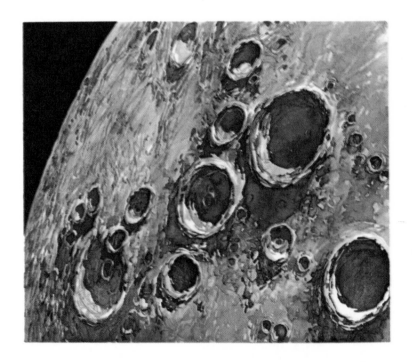

183

Man On The Moon

The First — This was a historic moment. On July 21, 1969, man set foot on the moon for the first time. It took years and years of study, experiments and tests before this great event was made possible. Thousands of people worked to build rockets and lunar modules to take the astronauts to the moon. Vast sums of money were spent in doing so. Some people died in accidents when the equipment was tested. But in the end, man's dream came true and now he is launching his spacecraft toward more distant stars and planets.

Dreams — Man has always dreamed of soaring through space to the moon. In past centuries, some people planned to reach it on a "plane" pulled by swans or in a balloon ship.

The Moon "Rocket" — A hundred years ago, Jules Verne wrote of reaching the moon in a shell-shaped wagon fired from a cannon.

Verne's imaginary rocket

Spacecraft — The first true spacecraft were not all that different, outwardly, from those described by Jules Verne. This is the first unmanned space probe, which brushed past the moon in 1959.

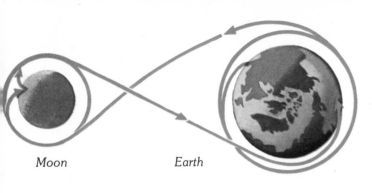

Moon   Earth

How They Traveled — Before reaching the moon, the astronauts first had to orbit the earth and then the moon itself.

Animals — Experimental flights using animals were made before men were launched into space. This is Laika, the famous Russian dog; it was the first dog to go into space.

The Great Day — When at last the scientists decided they were certain of success, man landed on the moon. Thanks to TV, the whole world was able to share in this event.

Laika, the canine astronaut

Space Walks — For practice, the first astronauts launched into orbit around the earth emerged from their spaceships wearing special clothing, to take a space walk or two.

Splashdown — Many trial runs were made of the reentry to earth and salvaging the craft with the astronauts inside.

Spacelabs — Before man ever set foot on the moon, spacelabs had been launched from the earth to provide scientists with information about our satellite. This spacelab on the surface of the moon is recording data.

On The Moon — A number of lunar vehicles were developed that could move easily over the moon's surface and explore it.

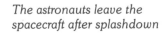

The astronauts leave the spacecraft after splashdown

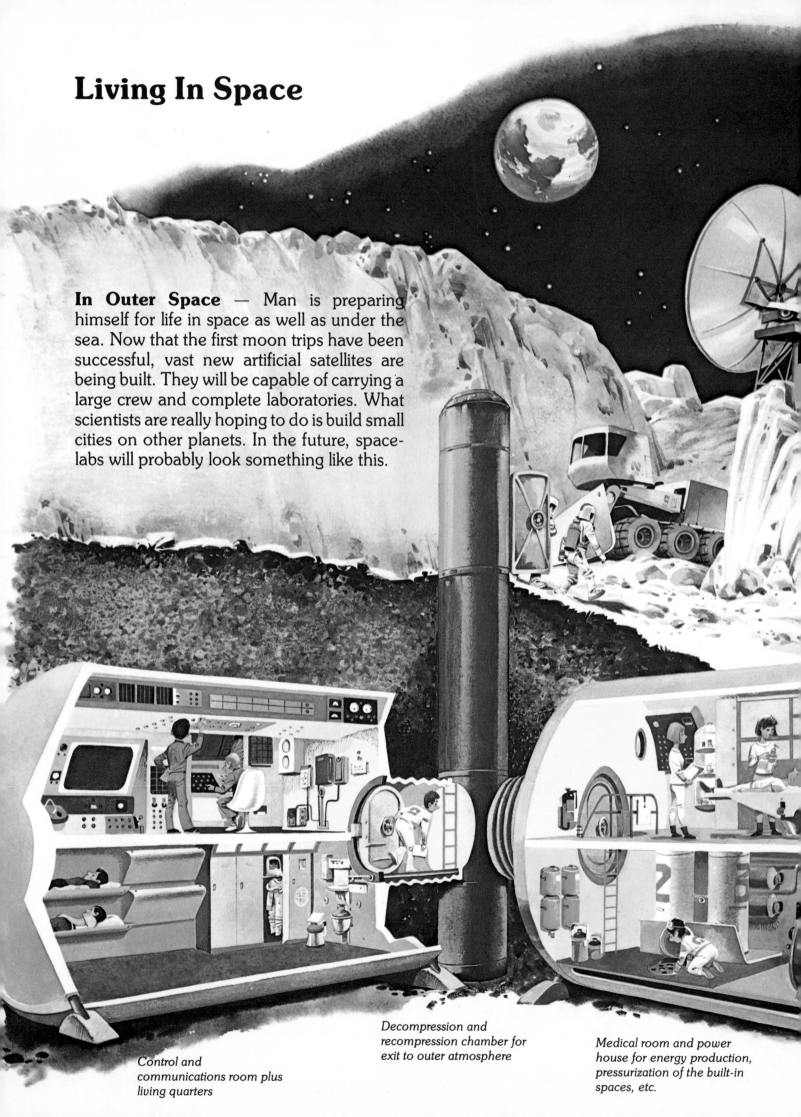

Living In Space

In Outer Space — Man is preparing himself for life in space as well as under the sea. Now that the first moon trips have been successful, vast new artificial satellites are being built. They will be capable of carrying a large crew and complete laboratories. What scientists are really hoping to do is build small cities on other planets. In the future, space-labs will probably look something like this.

Control and communications room plus living quarters

Decompression and recompression chamber for exit to outer atmosphere

Medical room and power house for energy production, pressurization of the built-in spaces, etc.

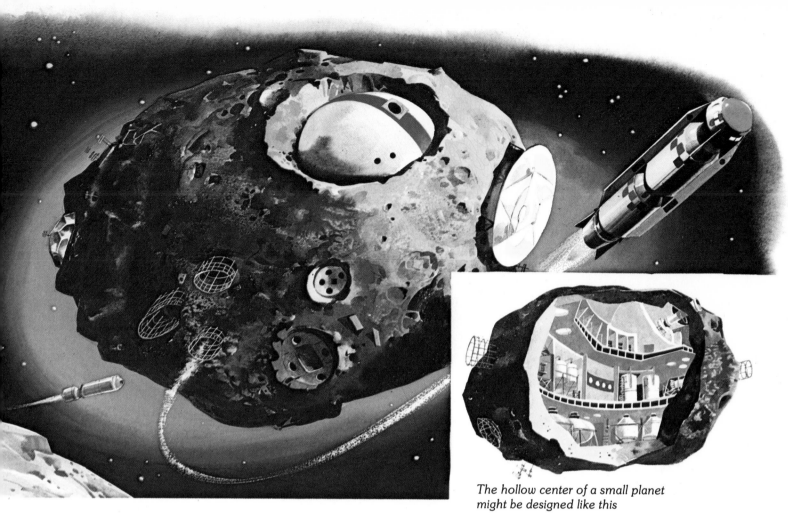

The hollow center of a small planet might be designed like this

Minor Planets — Some scientists hope that, one day in the future, one of the many smaller planets that rotate around the sun can be colonized along with the big planets. These little planets are masses of rock the size of mountains; they wander in space far from the earth. The picture shows how one of these smaller planets might be captured and turned into a spacelab and base.

Perfect Satellites — Before such conquests can be made, however, we will have to perfect the man-made satellites. Every kind of satellite is being built at the moment to carry out wonderful activities. Satellites send us pictures and sounds, control air and sea travel, forecast our weather, watch over every part of the earth's surface, tell us where plant life is diseased, and warn us of forthcoming earthquakes.

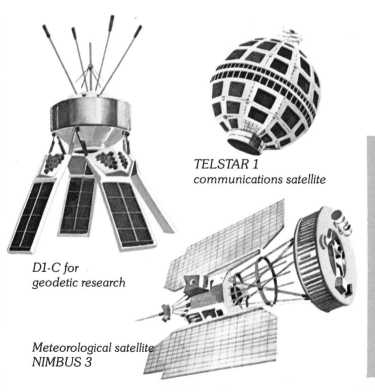

TELSTAR 1 communications satellite

D1-C for geodetic research

Meteorological satellite NIMBUS 3

Here are some practical uses for satellites (below)

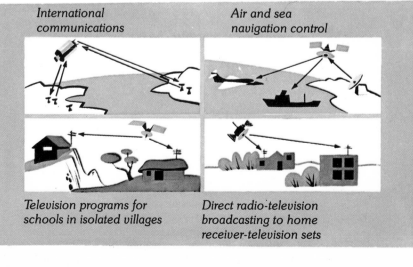

International communications

Air and sea navigation control

Television programs for schools in isolated villages

Direct radio-television broadcasting to home receiver-television sets

Index

191

ships, 125, 130, 133, 141, 167, 172, 173
shrimps, 105
Sierra Nevada, 88
signalling, 130
skeleton, 142
ski-lifts, 129
sky, 11, 76, 77, 79, 82
skyscrapers, 86, 165
slaves, 60
slings, 134
slush, 82
smelting, 55, 58, 59, 123, 124, 125, 129
snakes, 100, 101, 114, 115, 116, 117
snow, 82, 83, 102, 109
snowplow, 83
soccer, 162
solar, energy, 136, 137
   furnace, 136
   panels, 136, 137
   system, 10
sonar, 133
sound, 132, 133, 156, 157
South Pole, 83, 104, 105, 106, 107, 109
space, 10, 87, 178-187
spaceships, 137, 141, 178, 179, 184, 185
Spain, 70, 71, 93, 99
sparks, 128
spin dryer, 134
splitting the atom, 138
sponges, 18, 19, 31, 99
sports, 162, 163
springs, 79
squirrels, 27
starfish, 18, 19, 31
stars, 10, 131
steam, 11, 55, 122, 136, 167, 168
steamships, 122, 173
steel, 97, 125, 129
stems, 29
steppes, the, 110, 111
stings, 43, 121
stoves, 123
strata of rocks, 12, 14, 15
submarines, 107, 131, 138, 141, 167, 174, 175
sun, 10, 79, 136, 137, 140, 179
sundials, 144

sunlight, 24, 25, 93, 131
survival, struggle for, 48, 49
swallows, 76
Switzerland, 97

T
tadpoles, 32, 33
tar, 127
teddy bears, 119
telephone, 129, 158, 159
telescopes, 180, 181
television, 159, 160, 161, 185
temperature, 10, 11, 13, 14, 15, 82, 85
tennis, 162
tents, 111
termites, 118
Thermopylae, Battle of, 99
thorax, 40
tiger, 116, 117
timber, 28, 29, 56
time, 144, 145
tin, 59
toads, 32, 33
Tolltecs, 93
Toronto, 91
toucan, 46, 114, 115
tracks, animal, 82
traffic lights, 125, 130
trains, 141, 159
tram cars, 128
tree rings, 29
tree trunks, 28, 29
trees, 20-22, 24-26, 28, 41, 119
Triceratops, 17, 39
Trilobite, 16, 18
tropical rain forests, 114, 115
tunnels, 175
turnips, 22, 23
turtles, 121, 174

U
ultrasound, 133
United States of America, 74, 75, 86-89, 94
universe, the, 10, 178, 179

V
vacuum, 29
valleys, 11, 13, 97

Vatican City, 98
veins, 143
Venice, 65, 98, 145
Vercingetorix, 63
vibration, 132
Virginia, 74, 75
vocal chords, 132
volcanoes, 13, 14, 55, 92, 94, 183
Volta's pile, 128
vulture, 112

W
walls, 165
walrus, 102
Washington, DC, 86
Washington, George, 74, 75
wasps, 41
water, 78-81, 144, 167
waterholes, 112
water-wheels, 57, 167
weather, 76, 77, 82, 83
   forecasting, 76, 77, 187
weaving, 53
weeds, floating, 20
women's bowling, 163
whale, 36, 38, 103, 104
wheat, 29, 86, 90, 91
wheels, 56, 57
wild cat, 110
winches, 166
wind, 77, 84, 85, 110, 121, 166
windmills, 85, 98, 166
wolves, 110
woodcock, 46
wool, 52
worker bees, 43
worms, flat, 18
   peacock, 30
   polycheti, 18
writing, 146, 147

Y
Yellowstone National Park, 89
Yogi Bear, 89
Yorktown, Battle of, 75

Z
zebra, 112